KARL MARX

AND

BABASAHEB AMBEDKAR

A Comparative Study

KARL MARX
AND
BABASAHEB AMBEDKAR
A Comparative Study

R.K. Kshirsagar

KALPAZ

ISBN: 978-93-5128-098-9

Price: ₹ 660

First Published, 2015

Published by

Kalpaz Publications
C-30, Satyawati Nagar,
Delhi-110052
Ph. : 9212142040
E-mail: kalpaz@hotmail.com

Laser Typesetting : Awdesh, Delhi
Printed at : G. Print Process, Delhi

Cataloging in Publication Data—DK
Courtesy: D.K. Agencies (P) Ltd. <docinfo@dkagencies.com>

Kshirsagara, Ramchandra, 1945- **author.**
Karl Marx and Babasaheb Ambedkar : a comparative study / R.K. Kshirsagar.
pages cm
Includes bibliographical references (pages) and index.
ISBN 9789351280989

1. Ambedkar, B. R., 1891-1956.—Political and social views.
2. Marx, Karl, 1818-1883.—Political and social views. I. Title.

DDC 954.035 23

"Let the ruling classes tremble at a communistic revolution. The Proletarians have nothing to lose but their chains. They have a World to Win."

Karl Marx
(Manifesto of the
Communist Party, (1848)

* * * * * * * * * * * *

"The Depressed Classes should remember one thing that they have nothing to lose in this battle and everything to gain. They have only to shed the fear of death."

Dr. Babasaheb Ambedkar
(Pandharpur: 1937)

Contents

Photographs

Babasaheb Ambedkar

Karl Marx

Dr. Babasaheb Ambedkar

Born : 14th April, 1891 Parinirvan : 6th December, 1956

Karl Marx

Born : 5th May, 1818 Died on 14th March, 1883

Ramabai Ambedkar

Marx's wife : Jenny

Preface

It was my long cherished desire to present a comparative study of the thoughts and movements of the two great masters, Dr Karl Marx and Dr Babasaheb Ambedkar, in a book form. Today, I am happy to see that the book is being published.

Notwithstanding certain differences in their thoughts, approaches and strategies relating to the problem of liberation of the oppressed people, which could be attributable to the natural differences of their time, space and experiences, there was almost unanimity on their objective of liberation of the oppressed and suppresed. Both of them believed in the dialecticism, rationalism and scientific method of investigation of the remedies on the social problems. They had strenuously struggled throughout their life for the cause of the down trodden which was so dear to their tender heart. Both of them were of course, thinkers, activists as well as scholars to the core. It is generally a rare combination to be found in an individual; which needs to be analysed in proper way. They left the legacy of their rich, valuable and substantial contribution, having potential to inspire the oppressed people to raise their voice-against the oppressors. They had rightly advised the oppressed people to win political power for their upliftment, emancipation and amelioration.

However, it is awfully observed that there is dearth of comprative study of their vision and mission. It seems that the students of Marxism as well as Ambedkarism have not given much thought to this particular aspect of the study. I found that there are presently two books, one, *"Re-reading Ambedkar: Marxist - Ambedkarite Praxis"* (2007), written by

Thomas Mathew and other, *"Dr. Ambedkar Ani Marx* (1985- in Marathi) written by Raosaheb Kasabe, which deal with the subject specifically. I hope that in this backdrop, the readers would certainly appreciate my sincere efforts in presenting this work. Although, it is a specific work, it is succinct. Even there occurs repetition of some points; which could not be avoided in dealing with the subject. It is of course, based on original text written by both the thinkers and commentaries of eminent authors thereon. It is however based on rational and dispassionate interpretation without prejudice to any one.

In this venture, I am really indebted to several renowned authorities on the subject, who have enriched the present study. I am really grateful to principal S.R. Hanmante and Prof. S. S. Walde for having spared some of the valuable books from their personal library for my study. I am thankful to principal Sharad Adwant, Director, Swami Ramanand Teerth Research Institute, Aurangabad for having allowed me free access to the original source material at their disposal.

I am thankful to my son Deepak R. Kshirsagar (Asst. Professor of Law), who brought certain books to my knowledge. I would like to thank my wife Godavari R. Kshirsagar for her encouragement in my study. I must state that Samyak, Shubham and Medhavi have often given me pleasant trouble and constrained me to take a break in my study. I am thankful to Kotigre brothers for preparing the computerised copy of the manuscript.

I am thankful to the Kalpaz Publication for having published this book.

Dr. R.K. Kshirsagar

1

Introduction

It is true that Karl Marx and Babasaheb Ambedkar, the two great proponents of political theory are highly respected not only in their respective community and country, but in the humanity at large. They gave to the mankind a philosophy to revolt against the traditional society based on injustice and exploitation and the philosophy to reconstruct it on the sublime values of liberty, equality and fraternity. They were not only visionary but pragmatic activists to the core. They were worthy to be called compassionate emancipator of the suffering multitude.

1. It is, however necessary to comprehend and construe their emancipatory philosophy in the real prespective along with their intrinsic weaknesses, if any and with their strengths without any prejudice.
2. It is difficult to state as to how far Marxism and Ambedkarism doctrins are comparable in view of interception considerably of long time, space and cultural distance between them. However, there could be some scope for finding out the points of synthesis or similarities, if any in their philosophies and to come to some logical conclusion at the theoretical level.
3. In the growing process of privatisation, and globalisation at one hand and growing trend of communalism and terrorism at the other, there is utmost possibility of loss of human values including social justice. Therefore, it is imperative to be more conscious and deligent about that philosophy which could be able to fulfil the aspirations of oppressed and suppressed

classes in securing liberty, equality, fraternity and justice.

4. There seems to be much controversy between the two philosophies on the methodology of achieving their objectives. According to Karl Marx economic equality could be achieved only by force or bloody revolution. The new social order based on equality could be consolidated by dictatorship of the Proletariat. While Babasaheb Ambedkar thought that socio-economic equality could be achieved by constitutional methods and democratic government. It is, however necessary to analyse and interpret the facts and adhere to truth.
5. Another cause of contention is religion. Karl Marx thought that religion is opium. It is an instrument of exploitation in the hands of Bourgeoisie and the clergy serving no purpose. Hence, it must be abandoned. On the other hand Babasaheb Ambedkar said that religion based on blind faith, superstitions, and inequality ought to be discarded, but the religion, as a way of good-moral life ought to be accepted. Buddhism, being based on reason, morality and equality is necessary for human beings. Thus, both of them had the rationalist attitude towards the realm of religion. It is necessary to find out the respective social background on which both of them relied and reacted, and how they are nearer to each other in their views.
6. There is a greater confusion among the Indian intellengentia as to which philosophy could be more relevant in the present situation. Indian society is facing several problems like caste and intra-caste divisions, class and intra-class divisions, secular and non-secular forces, regional and sub-regional diversities, ethnic and minority divisions, gender inequality, superstitions, mal-administration etc. It is important to find the reasonable solutions on these vexed problems in the light of the philosophy of communism as well as in Ambedkarism and come to the conclusion about their relevance and relative value.

7. In other parts of the world the problem of racism, fundamentalism, terrorism and idealism are on rise due to lack of proper coordination and understanding, scientific outlook and respect for human values. In such a dilemma, it is appropriate to think of some common ideology which could be able to restructure the society on the true principles of liberty, equality, fraternity and justice. In addition to the formal organisation like UNO it would be worthwhile to develope a parallel philosophy to save the world community and its genuine interests.
8. It is equally important to take into account their vision as well as mission. Both the leaders were not only arm-chair thinkers, but they were active politicians. They were always with the people sharing their woes and grievances and assisting, consoling, encouraging and guiding, them in their venture. They were the vanguard of the people around them. They had to sacrifice their individual pleasure, family welfare and own prospects. It is necessary to put before the people their sacrificial example so that the people may try to emulate them.

In this backdrop, it is proposed:

1. to acquaint with the life and mission of Karl Marx and Babasaheb Ambedkar.
2. to know their doctrinal perception about the dialectical forces inherent in the society.
3. to study their thought in the context of society, religion and state, revolution, and socialism as a philosophy of social justice.
4. to know the essence of the creed of Karl Marx and the creed of Babasaheb Ambedkar and their contribution to the society.

Thus, the thoughts of Marx and Ambedkar were aimed to restructure the society free from exploitation. It is imperative to comprehend those thoughts in their real perspective and find viable solution on the present day problems in the light of their thoughts.

2

The Great Men

It is really difficult to draw a biographical sketch of the great revolutionary philosophers and compassionate activists, who by the dint of missionary zeal, unflinching determination and ceaseless endeavours properly moulded the biographies of the innumerable people, like Karl Marx and Babasaheb Ambedkar. So, it is important to present the glimpses of their life succinctly so as to acquainting with them for the greater understanding of their vision and mission.

(a) *Karl Marx : (1818-1883)*

Karl Marx was born on 5th May 1818 at Trier in the State of Prussia in Germany. It is in the vicinity of Rhineland which was under the influence of two great cultures.

German and French. The Rhine province was an industrially developed regions of Prussia. His father Herr Herinrich Marx (1782-1838) was by profession a barrister at the Higher Court of Appeal at Trier. His mother Henriettee Presborck was housewife. They were well to do. They had a two-storeyed house at 664, Brucken grasse. Heinrich Marx was well known and respected in his town and vicinity for his legal expertise, high moral standard and helping nature.

Heinrich Marx was a Jewish by faith, but later on he adopted Lutheranism in 1824. "At that time," according to Franz Mehring, "the renunciation of Judaism was not an act of religious emancipation, but also and even more so, an act of social emancipation". It was, "an entrance card into the community of European Culture."[1] There was a pleasant and liberal ambience at his house. He had maintained cordial relations with Christian Saints, Barons and Elites.

Marx's family was friendly with that of Privy Counsellor Baron Ludwig Von West Phalen, whose family was highly influential in the region of Prussia. Their close relation culminated into Kinship relation as Jenny (1814-1881), daughter of Baron Ludwig was married to Karl Marx.

Karl Marx was extremly fond of his father who inspired him to work for the cause of society always. He made him to read, grasp and comprehend Voltaire, Racine, Homer, Shakespeare and Saint Simon, and enriched his understanding of knowledge.

Karl Marx completed his early education in his native town, Trier from 1830 to 1835. He completed his matriculation in October 1836. Karl was by no means regarded as a brilliant pupil. His marks in all subjects were mediocre, the lowest one given by his teachers.[2] In his school days Karl studied gymnasium, mathematics etc. In 1835 Marx, went to study Law at Bonn University; and at Berlin University. In 1841 Karl Marx obtained his degree of Doctor of philosophy at the University of Jena, on the subject, "The difference between the natural philosophy of Democritus and Epicurus." "Amongst the older natural philosophers of Greece," in the words of Mehring, "Democritus was the one who had adhered most closely to materialism. Out of nothing, nothing can come. Nothing that is can be destroyed. All change is nothing but the joining and separation of parts. Nothing happens fortuitously and everything that happens, happens with reason and necessity. Nothing exists but the atoms and empty space, everything else is opinion. The atoms are endless in number and of an infinite variety in form. Falling eternally through infinite space the larger atoms, which fall more quickly, collide with the smaller atoms, and the material movements and rotations which result are the begining of the formation of worlds. Innumerable worlds form and pass away, co-existently and successively."

"Epicurous took over this conception of nature from Democritus, but he made certain alterations. The famous of the alterations consisted in the so called swerve of the atoms." Epicurous contended that in their fall the atoms "swerved", that is to say, that they did not fall vertically but in a deviation from the straight line.

"Naturally, Marx did not deny the physical unreasonableness of the Epicurian phisolophy and he condemned," the reckless irresponsibility of Epicurus in the explanation of physical phenomena,. "He pointed out that the only test of truth for Epicurus was the evidence of senses: Epicurus believed the diameter of the sun to be two feet because it looked so to his eyes. However, Marx did not content himself with dismissing these evident absurdities with a phrase or two, but set himself to trackdown the philosophic reason in the physical unreason."

"Democritus concerned himself exclusively with material existence of the atom, whereas Epicurus concerned himself further with the atom as a conception, with its form as well as its matter, with its essence as well as its existence. Epicurean regarded the atom as being not only the material basis of the world of phenomona, but also the symbol of the isolated individual, the formal principle of abstract individual self-consciousness."

"In this his first work Marx reveals himself as a constructive thinker, even if one contests the details of his interpretation of the Epicurean philosophy."[3]

Karl Marx was a rationalist and radical activist. He was in a opposition camp to the Prussian Government and the other feudal authorities. He would have been appointed as a University Teacher, but because of his liberal views, the university authorities suspected him of his fidelity and loyality to the State. Therefore, Marx entered the field of journalism for his livelihood.

He joined the office of *"Rheinisene Zeitung,"* in April 1842 and became its editor in October of the same year. "He launched a bold campaign against the regime of social, political and spiritual oppression which prevailed in Prussia and throughout Germany."[4]

According to Stepanova, "His experience on the paper gave Marx better knowledge of political life in Germany and the conditions of the working people. Numerous facts of the heartless attitude of the Prussian Government and its officials to the vital needs of the people led Marx to the conclusion that this Government, its officials and its laws reflected and upheld not the interests of the people, but those of the ruling estates : The nobility and priesthood."[5] However, due to censorship he had to resign from the service of the Zeitung from 1st April 1843.

Karl Marx, however had not given prime importance to his profession. Marx challenged the philistine ideal of personal well being as a motto in life. He thought very rightly that, "If he (a person) works only for himself he may perhaps become a famous man of learning, a great sage, an excellent poet, but he can never be a perfect, truly greatman."[6] The main object of his life was "work for mankind."[7]

His choice as a life partner fell on Baroness Jenny Von Westphalen. In 1843, Marx married to Jenny, daughter of Freiherr Ludwig Von Westphalen. "She was four years older than Karl-Marx, but still only in the early twenties."[8] "Jenny had to share with her husband all the burden of his restless life; wandering, prison, emigration, poverty and savage persecution. Three of her children died. But she was Marx's closest associate and counsellor his good genie. She lived to see Marx's name become the symbol of tho now, fighting world from

Russia to America, and this compensated for everything."[9]

"Jenny was not only a wife to him, but his closest friend and counsellor and the first critic of his works... He admired Jenny's literary talent and considered her a real virtuoso in the epistolary art."[10] For many years she was his secretary. "She conducted a correspondence with many active figures in the international working class movement and took a great interest in everything connected with this movement. She regarded herself proudly as a party worker."[11]

"In the Marx's house, in spite of the extremely modest life-style, political exiles always found refuge, help and comfort."[12] Jenny did not simply share in her husbands fate toil and struggle but actively participated in all three with the fullest awareness and the warmest of ardour."[13]

When Karl Marx was very busy with writing *'Capital'*, he lost time, money and health. Therefore, he had to work with the American *Newyork Daily Tribune* for some modest income. He had to suffer a lot, "when Marx's little daughter died in 1852 there was not even enough money for her burial."[14]

In the words of Genrikh Volkov, "the years passed, but poverty continued to dog Marx and his family. In 1861, Marx lost his work for the newspaper, his main source of income. Sometimes he did not go outside for weeks, because his clothes were in pawn. Putting aside his economic calculations for capital, he would draw up endless lists of debts to the baker, butcher, landlord.... The *"Terrible"* head of the first infernational was often compelled to hide from his creditors whom he regarded as monsters."[15] In 1862, Marx wrote to Engels, "My wife tells mc every day that it would be better if she and the children were in the grave, and I really can not blame her for it; because the humiliations, torments and horrors which have to be endured in this situation are really indescribable."[16]

This destitution has amply reflected in the letter written by Karl Marx's wife, Jenny to her friend. She states that, "Let me describe only one day of this life, as it actually was, and you will see that perhaps few other refugees have had to suffer as much. Since wet-nurses are exceedingly expensive here, I made up my mind, despite terrible pains in the breasts and the back to nurse the baby myself. But the poor little angel drank in so much sorrow with the milk that he was continually pretting, in violent pain day and night. Since he has been in the world, he has not slept a single night through, at most two or three hours. Of late, there had been violent spasms, so that the child is continually betwixt life and death.....one day I was sitting (nursing the poor dear) when our landlady suddenly appeared. In the course of the winter, we had paid her more than two hundred and fifty thalers, and then it had been agreed that in future we were not to pay her but her landlord, who had put in an execution. Now, she repudiated, this agreement,and demanded the five pounds which we still owed her. Since we could not pay this sum instantly, two brokers came into the house and took possesion of all my belongings—bedding, clothes, everything, even the baby's cradle and the little girl's toys, so that the children wept bitterly. They threatened to take every thing away in two hours. If this had happened, I should have had to lie on the floor, with my freezing children beside me, and with my aching breast. Our friend Schramm hastened forthwith to seek help. He took a cab, the horses fell down; he jumped out and was brought back into the house bleeding, the house where I was lamenting and my poor children were Trembling."[17] When Karl Marx was deported from Belgium, Jenny was not knowing this fact, nor the whereabouts of Karl Marx. Therefore, she went to know about him to the police station. The police without knowing her identity, took her in custody for a night and kept her with prostitutes and bad characters. She was not only to live in utter poverty with Marx, but had to face unbearable pains and agony.

Jenny had to live in slum area of London in a two-room rented house and urgrudgingly she lived with Marx happily despite facing lot of hardships. She was happy in the company of Marx; Although she did not get that much comfort which she got in her parent's house. Even, when their daughter expired due to bronchitis is, they had no sufficient money to take her to burial ground.[18]

Marx was, "The thick-set man with his broad forchead and dark flashing eyes, his jet-black hair and full beard immediately attracted general attention."[19].

His father Heinrich Marx died in 1839, and his mother Henriette died in 1863. Having seen the wrtched condition of Marx, his parents were unhappy. His mother "used to say bitterly that he would have done better to acquire some capital get more money some other way instead of writing a book about it."[20]

At the end of October 1843, Marx went to Paris. "Life in the French capital enriched him with new knowledge and political experience. He was a frequent visitor to the outskirts of the city where the workers lived. He made contacts with the leaders of the league of the Just, a secret society of German workers and artisans, and also with the leaders of most of the French secrete societies, without however, joining any of them."[21]

The appearance of the Manifesto which coincided with the bourgeois democratic revolution in France in February 1848, that was echoed in other countries of Europe as well. The Belgian government, alarmed at the growth of the revolutionary movement. They arrested Marx and deported him.[22] He left for Paris in order to take part in the revolutionary struggle.

The new Rheinische Zeitung, founded by Marx and Engels, unfurled the banner of democracy. The first issue of Zeitung (new) appeared on 1st June 1848.[23]

He was charged with anti-national activities, but acquitted by the Jury in Cologne. Later, on 13th June, 1849 the Government issued a deportation order against Marx. Hence, he left for London on 24th August 1849.[24]

In his days of exile in London, "Marx was in the habit of speaking, thinking and writing in three European languages: German, English and French. He was also conversant with Italian and Spanish".[25]

Engels happened to meet Karl Marx in the latters office of the Rheinische Zeitung at Cologue in 1842. This meeting of two hearts remained alive for lifelong. Engels and Marx, both came to England and Engels settled in Manchester and worked as a clerk in the office of a Cotton Mill. Engels helped his friend Marx by his moral and material co-operation. Lenin writes, "Had it not been for Engel's constant and selfless financial aid, Marx would not only have been unable to complete Capital but would have inevitably been crushed by want."[25(a)]

Karl Marx, by completing Volume-1 of Capital in August 1867, writes to Engels that, "So this volume is finished. It was thanks to you alone that this became possible. Without your self sacrifice for me I could never possibly have done the enormous work for the three volumes. I embrace you, full of thanks...! Greetings, my dear, beloved friend !"[25(b)]

Karl Marx was not only a philosopher, but a pragmatic activist. The main objective of his life was to abolish the class-structure of the society and to establish an egalitarian society. He founded the Communist party and led it through out his life and became successful in spreading it in most of the parts of the world.

"Firstly, he organised the small cells of the Communist party, called Communist League and gave, a clear programme for the reorganisation of society." The Communist League was an organisation of the Proletariat purported to organise the Communist movement and lead the Communist revolution a new dimension. Its programme or the "Communist Manifesto" was approved by the Proletariat in the conference of the communist league held in London in November 1847. It was, however against the established ruling class and the feudal lords. The Communist League, led the class war, in France in 1848; but in vain. Therefore, it had to work underground and tolerate persecution and ultimately it was banned.

Secondly, they formed 'the working men's International Association, in place of Communist League, on September 28, 1864 in London. It was also dissolved after almost nine years of its formation in 1874. Although the 'International Assocfiations' lived for a short period, its work proved to be substantial and monumental.

Marx and Engels spread the Communist movement in Germany, France, England, Italy, Russia, Poland and Switzerland with great zeal, determination and sacrifices.

Thus we find a great blend of thought and activism in the life of Karl Marx. His heart was melted to see the unbearable pains and agony of the proletariat class. Therefore, he was inclined to work for the betterment of the working men and women. "His life in politics" as observed by volkov, "was inseparable from his life in science, one sphere of activity fertilised and stimulated the other. And in both he fought equally mercilessly for the purity of ends and means, considering all deviations from this as shameful."[26]

Jenny, the life partner of Karl Marx breathed her last in 1881. Karl Marx and Jenny Marx had four daughters, first was Jenny, born in May 1844, second was Laura, born in September 1845, third was Franziska, born in 1851 and fourth was Eleanaur, born in 1855. They had two sons, first was Edgar, born in 1847, and second was Heinrich Guido, born in 1849.

However, Franziska died in 1852 when she was only one year old; Heinrich Guido also died of pneomonia in 1850 within one year of age and Edgar, his loving son died in 1855 at his eighth year, in 1855.

Jenny, Laura and Eleanor all became active in the communist movement. Laura married Paul Lafargue in 1868 and became his true aide in the revolutionary struggle. Jenny married Charles Longuet in 1872, a prominent leader of the International. Eleanor married Edward in 1884, after her father's death.

(*a*) *Influences and Inspirations*:

Every thought has its dialectic origin. No thought could be either fully independent or isolated from other. Every thought is subject to anti-thesis and culmination into synthesis. Every thought or idea has potential to generate some waves in the society. The thinkers generally react either by substantiating or contradicting the given ideas depending on their utility and vitality. In other words, every thinker is generally influenced and inspired by the preceding or prevailing ideas.

"A hundred years ago there was a man in Germany named Karl Mavx, who wrote so much and so well about communism that a great many people think he invented it. He did not. There were communists before Marx; and still earlier, before anyone had thought of calling them communists, there were people who hold the same kind of belief."[27]

It is, however difficult to find out who actually influenced Kar Marx. He had not admitted expressly to that effect. The critics and commentators of his thought, however stated in ambiguous terms regarding his preceptors. Karl Marx refers to some thinkers in his writings, but not with gratitude. He comments on them as 'utopian.'

However, his debt could be traced by referring to critical appreciation of some ideas and some similarities with the preceding thought.

(1) *Adam Smith (1723-1790)*: He highlights the importance of labour power and labour contribution to the augmentation of the wealth of nation. He thought that the state must adhere to the philosophy of Laissez-faire and to the perfectly competitive market. He thought that the national wealth lies not in foreign trade or in land but in labour. Labour is the real measure of the exchangeable value of all commodities; and money is a convenient medium of exchange. According to him, division of labour gives rise to opulance and it is beneficial.[28]

(2) *Immanual Kant (1724-1804)* : Karl Marx was indebted to "Following Rousseau, Kant announced that man was the end in himself of social development and not a means of attaining other ends."[29] He developed the ideas of sovereignty of the people's power and the equality of all in law. However, he believed that private property is essential for the development of human personality. He believed that constitutional monarchy is the best form of Government and opposed to revolution. He thought that the state is the creation of self-conscious reason. Law is based on morality, as such command has no place. Marx also gave importance to individual development.

(3) *Saint Simon (1760-1825)* : He said that the new social order would consist of manual workers, live agriculturists, artisans, manufacturers, bankers, savants and artists. Each member was to draw benefits from the common pool in proportion to his stake in the state." The principle, viz., to each according to his contribution, was parallel to the later socialist principle in which the rule was to each according to his needs."[30]

(4) *Johann Fichte (1762-1814)* : According to "Individuals should be viewed in the context of their social existence. They are parts of the socicty which is an organism in itself and therefore individuals as individuals have no rights."[31] According to Genrikh Volkov, "The young Marx, who himself thirsted for action and longed to make

scientific thought a fire and sword to change the world, obtained a great deal in his early student years from the philosophy and outlook of Fichte."[32] Further, he states that, Marx was not fully satisfied with the philosophy of Kant and Fichte. "Marx longs to have a theoretical understanding not only of the Trichotomy of the "spirit" but also of what is taking place "in the street" in real life."[33]

(5) *Ludwig Feuerbach (1762-1814)* : He was a pioneer of the nineteenth century materialist revival because of whom Marx connected dialectic with materialistic view. His thoughts inspired Marx to go ahead with his thinking. In the words of Yuri Sdobnikov, "Marx was also attracted to Feuerbach because of his own ideas about the earthly origins of religion."[34]

(6) *George Wilhelm Friedrich Hegel (1770-1831)*: He thought that history is the unfolding of absolute reason, and the principle of historical evolution was dialectic.[35] According to Hegel 'idea' determines our institutions. However Marx replaced 'idea' by 'matter' and said that it is not 'idea' or intelligence, but the material condition which is the basis of all the super structure. Thus, Karl Marx developed the theory of materialist interpretatin of history in place of Hegelian idealistic interpretation of history. The individual and the state are not opposed to one another.

(7) *Robert Owen (1771-1858)* : He was owner and manager of a Mill which employed about two thousand workers. He established co-operative stores for the mill workers. He thought that labour and capital should work in harmony with instead of confronting each other. He was of the view that some kindness should be shown to the labourers. It was wrong to think that payment of low wages is profitable to the capitalists. He thought that paying higher wages to labourers was necessary so that they may maintain their health and efficiency. He had forbidden to employ children under ten years in his Mill.

He provided for free and regular education to the children of the labourers. He provided model dwelling and reduced number of daily working hours. Even he proposed to limit the profit to only five per cent of their investment. However, his proposal of reducing profit was not acceptable to his partners. Ultimately, he dissolved his partnership for the cause of labourers. He opposed to class-struggle and strikes.

He advocated to establish co-operative communities, which people could join on voluntary basis and share the work of production, on no profit, no money and each person would work according to his ability and training and all would share the goods produced. Thus, he propogated the principle of modern socialism. Therefore he was considered, "the father of British Socialism."[36]

(8) *Sismondi (1773-1842)* : He was "a precursor of socialism." The industrial revolution during his time caused misery to the working class and over production, because of which there arose economic crisis. Therefore, he thought that, "the revival of peasant proprietorship in agriculture and the return of the independent artisan in industry would eliminate the frightful sufferings arising from the industrial revolution."[37] He thought that the economic activity has to be judged from the point of view of its effects on human welfare. Therefore, he regarded the problem of the distribution of wealth as more important than any other economic problems.

(9) *Charles Fourier (1772-1837)* : He wanted to attain the plan of socialism by peaceful means and by small experiments; like "Phalansteres." "These 'Phalansteres' would be both consumers and producers co-operatives in which the rights of labour capital and ability would be recognised".[38] Accordingly, each member of the Phalansteres would receive a minimum of subsistance from the produce or profit and the remaining part would be divided in shares depending on the members

contributions, five twelths to labour, four twelfth to capital and three twelths to the managing talents. He however wanted to improve the position of the worker by making him a share holder in the said co-operatives. He wanted to overcome the evils of industrialisation by such organisational units in rural areas. Marx, however categorised him as utopian socialist.[39]

(*b*) *His Writings*:

Karl Marx was a prolific writer. He wrote certain thought-provoking books. They are:

S. *No.*	*Titles*	*Written*	*Published*
1.	The Holy Family or Critique of Critical Criticism	1845	1845
2.	Theses on Feuerbach	1847	1888
3.	The Poverty of Philosophy	1847	
4.	Manifesto of the Communist Party	1847	1848
5.	A contribution to the Critique of Hegels' Philosophy of Law	1843	1927
6.	Difference between the Democritean and Epicurean Philosophy of nature.		1902
7.	A Contribution to the Critique of Political Economy		1902
8.	Das Capital (Vol. I)		1867
9.	Das Capital (Vol. II)		1885
10.	Das Capital (Vol.III)		1894
11.	Revolution and Counter Revolution		

He tried to start a radical journal entitled 'Archiv des theeismus' with the help of Bruno Bauer in 1841. However, he could not be successful in his plan.

Besides, he composed ballads, sonnets and poems. He was given the work of writing two articles in a week, for the American New York Daily Tribune. He got some amount for his subsistence. In 1861, Marx lost his work for the newspaper which was his main source of income.[40]

Karl Marx was however born in a well-to-do family and grown-up in a morally, materially culturally developed family. However, due to his love and compassion for poor proletariat class and utmost zeal to do something for them compelled him to abnegate all comforts of life. He eventually died in a very poor and wretched condition in England on 14th March 1883. Pity is that very few persons were present at his funeral.

[B] *Babasaheb Ambedkar* : (1891-1956)

Dr. Bhimrao Ramji Ambedkar, popularly known as 'Babasaheb', was born on April 14, 1891 at Mhow in the vicinity of Indore[41] in Madhya Pradesh. His father's name was Ramji and mother's name was Bhimabai. His ancestral village was Ambadhave located in Mandangarh taluka in the district of Ratnagiri in Maharashtra. He belonged to an untouchable *mahar* community. He came of a valiant and cultured family. His father Ramji was in the British Army. His grandfather Maloji was also in the British Army. His mother belonged to Murbad village in Thana district in Maharashtra, and her family also had the tradition of Military service.

At the time of his birth his father Ramji was serving as Head Master in Military school at Mhow and attained the rank of Subedar Major. He retired from his service when Bhim was two years old. After retirement from military service his father came to Dapoli in Ratnagiri district in 1894. Soon his father was appointed as storekeeper in Ratnagiri and later on transferred to Satara in the year 1896. Later on his family shifted to Bombay in 1904, and lived in a room in Dabak Chawl at lower parel. He had two brothers, Balaram and

Anandrao and two sisters, Manjula and Tulsa. His mother expired in his early childhood at Satara. Therefore, his aunt (father's sister) named Meerabai took care of him.

Babsaheb's father was a staunch follower of Kabir Panth. He used to read and recite devotional songs of saint poet Chokha Maharaj and Tukaram Maharaj. He used to read Bhagwat Geeta, Ramayana and Mahabharata. He was a teetotaller and vegetarian. He was economically poor, but maintained cleanliness, discipline and religious atmosphere in the family to the core.

His original surname was Sankpal.[42] However, it was changed to 'Ambavadekar' on the name of his village. It was further changed to 'Ambedkar' by his teacher named 'Ambedkar' who loved Bhim in his school days.

Bhimrao completed his primary education at Satara in 1904. Then he was admitted to Elphinston High School, Bombay where from he had completed his matriculation in 1907. He passed his B.A. in 1913 from Elphinston college, Bombay.[43] Then with the kind help of Maharaja Sayajirao Gaikwad of Baroda, he went to pursue his further education in the famous Columbia University, New York in July 1913.[43(a)] He was awarded M.A. in Economics in June 1915 on his thesis, *"Ancient Indian Commerce."* Simultaneously, he continued his research leading to Ph.D. He submitted his thesis, *"National Divident of India* - A Historic and Analytical Study", to the Columbia University in June 1916 on which he obtained Ph.D Degree.

His thirst for knowledge was not quenched. He went to London and joined there in London School of Economics and Politics in October 1916. He was awarded M.Sc. on his thesis, "Provincial Decentralisation of imperial finance in British India," in June 1921. He was awarded D.Sc. on his thesis, "The Problem of Rupee", in 1923. He studied from morning to evening in the British

Museum Libray and India Office Library. In the meantime, he joined Gray's Inn and completed Barrister-at-Law.

Later, on June 6, 1952 the Columbia University, New York awarded him LL.D. in his honour being successful architect of the Constitution of India. The Osmania University, Hyderabad also honoured him by awarding D.Lit on January 12, 1953.

Babasaheb married to Ramabai daughter of Bhiku Walangkar resident of Dapoli in Ratnagiri. In the marriage Bhim was 14 years old and Ramabai was of 9 years old. Her father was a poor labourer belonging to mahar community. Ramabai was illiterate. She managed her family within a meagre amount and maintained very healthy atmosphere in the family. She died on May 27, 1935 due to ill health. Ramabai gave birth to Yeshwant in 1916. Later on Gangadhar their second son was born sometime in 1920 and expired when he was two and half years old. Later Ramesh was born but he also died in his infancy. Indu was their only daughter, she also died in her infancy. Their last child Rajratna was born in June 1924. Rajratna was also died in his infancy in 1926. They could not get proper treatment due to poverty. Their only surviving son by name Yeshwant lived irrespective of his ill health. He led the Ambedkarite movement throughout his life.

Later on after thirteen years of the death of his first wife, Dr. Babasaheb Ambedkar on medical ground married Dr. Sharada Kabir, a Saraswat Brahmin lady doctor, on April 15, 1948 at New Delhi.

After returning to India he joined as a Lieutenent in the Baroda State Forces in 1913. When he came to know that his father was serious, he came to Bombay within a few days of joining the service. However, his father breathed his last before his arrival to Bombay. Then he did not go to Baroda to join the service as he was frustrated to face acute untouchability threat. Again, when he returned after taking higher education in USA and UK in July 1917, he joined the Maharaja's service at Baroda as a Military Secretary. It was obligatory on his part to serve the Baroda state for a period of ten years as per bond signed by him as a pre-condition for obtaining the grant of scholarship for pursuing higher studies in foreign land.[44] Again, he was subjected to discriminations on the ground of untouchability by the staff in the department. He could not get residential accommodation also. Therefore, he had to leave the service in November 1917. He returned to Bombay.

Bhimrao was appointed as a professor of political economy in Sydenham College, Bombay on November 11, 1918. He resigned his professorship on March 11, 1920. Again he went to London in September 1920 to complete his study. He was there till 1923.

After returning from England, he started his legal practice at the Bombay High Court in June 1923. From June 1925 to March 1928, he served as a part-time teacher in Mercantile Law in Batliboi's Accountancy Training Institute, Bombay. From June 1928 to March 1929, he served as a professor of law in Government Law College, Bombay. He served as principal of the same college from June 1935 to June 1938. Thereafter, he resumed his full-time legal practice and socio-political work till his last.

He started his mission from 1919. On January 27, 1919 he gave evidence before the South Borough Committee on franchise and strongly advocated for separate electorate with reserved seats in the legislature for the Depressed Classes.[45] In order to bring socio-political awakening to the Depressed Classes, he started 'Mook Naik'[46] (Leader of the Dumb) a fortnightly in Marathi from Bombay on January 31, 1920. It continued till 1923. He appeared at first before the untouchable masses in a conference held at Mangaon near Kolhapur on 21 March 1920. He presided over the conference and the Maharaja of Kolhapur, Shahu Chhatrapati addressed to the conference.

The first All India Conference of the Depressed Classes was held at Nagpur on May 30, 31 and June 1, 1920. It was presided over by Chhatrapati Shahu Maharaj and Dr. Babasaheb Ambedkar, among others addressed to the conference. It was attended by delegates from Bombay, C.P. and Berar, Madhyaprant, Madras and Bengal. The conference resolved, among others, to have true representatives of the Depressed Classes in the legislature.[47]

After spending two and half years from September 1920 to February 1923 in England for higher studies, he returned to India and resumed his mission. In order to institutionalise the socio-political activities for the emancipation of the Depressed Classes, he formed one *"Bahishkrit Hitakarini Sabha"* (Depressed classes welfare organisation), on July 20, 1924 at Bombay.[48] Its president was Sir Chimanlal Setalvad, managing committee chairman was Babasaheb Ambedkar and its Secretary was S.N. Shivtarkar. The sabha started one hostel at Sholapur for high school students belonging to the depressed classes on January 4, 1925. The management of the hostel was entrusted to Shri Jivappa Subha Aydale, a social worker from Sholapur.

He was nominated to the Bombay Legislative Council with effect from February 18, 1927 for a period of five years. He was renominated in 1932 for a period of five years.

In order to assert the right to equality, he undertook a unique *satyagraha* at the famous Chowdar Tank at Mahad, alongwith his followers, on March 20, 1927. They burnt *Manusmriti* at Mahad on December 25, 1927 as a protest against inequality provided under it.[49] During this period he started *Bahishkrit Bharat,* a fortnightly[50] on April 3, 1927. It continued upto November 15, 1929. He formed *Samaj Samata Sangh* (Social Equality

Organization) on September 4, 1927 and Samata Sainik Dal (Equality Volunteer Army) in December 1927 to bring a new vigour and militancy to the March of equality.

He introduced the Bill No. XII of 1928 to amend the Bombay Hereditary Offices Act, 1874, in the Bombay Legislative Council on March 19, 1928. Again, he introduced the Bill to that effect in the Bombay Legislative Assembly (Bill No. XXIII of 1937) on September 17, 1937. The objects of the said Bill were: (1) to make the better provisions for the remuneration of the watandars, (2) to allow commutation of watans. (3) to free the inferior watandars from the obligation to serve the ryots; and (4) to define the duties of officiating watandars. Moreover, he introduced the Bill No. XX of 1937 to abolish the Khoti system in the Bombay Legislative Assembly, on September 17, 1937. The main objective of this Bill was to abolish the exploitative Khoti system prevailing in Konkan area and give the inferior holders the status of occupants. However, these bills were not passed by the Bombay Legislature in those days.[51]

When the Indian Statutory Commission under Sir John Simon came to India, he submitted the statement on May 29, 1928 on behalf of the Depressed Classes and gave evidence on October 23, 1928. He demanded adult franchise, joint electrorate and reserved seats for the depresed classes. However, the Commission did not take due cognizance of his demands.

He founded Depressed Classes Education Society, Bombay in June 14, 1928. The Bombay Government accorded sanction to five hostels, established at Panvel, Thane, Nasik, Pune and Dharwad by the society for the special benefit of high school students belonging to the Depressed Classes.[52]

In order to assert the right to religion and religious equality Ambedkar launched the temple entry *satyagraha* at Kalaram Temple, Nasik, on March 2, 1930.[53] The *satyagraha* was in continuation of course intermitantly for a period of five years; but in vain. It ultimately culminated into the famous declaration by him to renounce Hinduism, at Yeola on October 13, 1935.

In the meantime he presided over the All India Depressed Classes Congress held at Nagpur on August 8 and 9, 1930. The conference reposed its faith in the leadership of Dr. Babasaheb Ambedkar.[54] The second All India Depressed Classes Congress was held on May 7 and 8, 1932 at Kamathi, near Nagpur. It was presided over by R.B. Muniswami Pillai of Madras. L.N. Hards presented welcome address. Dr. Babasaheb Ambedkar, R.B. Srinivasan, R.L. Biswas, Swami Achhutanand, M.B. Mullick, Hansraj, N.C. Dhusia and many others addressed the conference. The conference accepted the leadership of Dr. Babasaheb Ambedkar and reiterated the demands put before the round table conference by Babasaheb Ambedkar and R.B. Srinivasan. The conference at the end elected as All India working committee in which R.B. Muniswami Pillai was elected president, R.L. Biswas as General Secretary and T.C. Sakhare and Rai Saheb Ram Sahai as its joint Secretaries.[55]

In order to discuss and decide the nature of future Constitution of India, and resolve the communal problem, the British government convened the Round Table Conferences in London, and invited, among others, Dr. Babasaheb Ambedkar and R.B.R. Srinivasan as representatives of the Depressed Classes to the said conferences. This was, of course the first occasion when the British government recognised the Depressed Classes as a separate element in Indian Politics, which could be rightly attributed to the strenuous efforts of Dr Babasaheb Ambedkar. He, however, participated in the Round Table Conferences, first from November 12, 1930 to January 19, 1931, second from September 7, 1931 to December 1, 1931 and

Third from November 17, 1932 to December 24, 1932. The British government conceded the demand of separate electorate to the Depressed Classes putforth by Babasaheb Ambedkar in the first and second conference. However, due to Mahatma Gandhi's epic fast in its opposition he had to accept 'Poona Pact 1932' which envisaged joint electorate with reserved seats.[56] During this period, he submitted his note to the Indian Franchise Committee, known as Lothian Committee, on May 1, 1932.

Once again he started one fortnightly, namely *'Janata'* [57] (the people) on November 24, 1930. It became weekly from October 31, 1931 and it was renamed as Prabuddha Bharat from February 4, 1956.

In order to protect the political interests of the Scheduled Castes and other weaker sections, he founded the Independent Labour Party on August 15, 1936. When general elections were declared under the Act of 1935, he fielded his candidates on certain reserved and non-reserved seats in the Bombay Presidency and in C.P. and Berar. He contested from Bombay (East) reserved constituency. The other contestants to the same seat were Baloo Palvankar (Cong.), P.N. Rajbhoj and Deorukhkar. Dr Babasaheb Ambedkar was declared to have been elected on February 17, 1937. He took very active interest in the proceedings of the Legislative Assembly. However, the Assembly was prorogued in 1939 in the wake of the outbreak of the second world War.

When the Industrial Trade Dispute Bill virtually banning the strike was introduced in the Bombay Legislature in September 1938, near about sixty labour unions declared to launch token strike for a day on November 7, 1938 in protest against the said Bill.[58] Dr Babasaheb Ambedkar also actively participated in the strike along with other labour unions.

He founded at the first national level political party called All India Scheduled Castes Federation in the special convention held at Nagpur on July 18-20, 1942. R.B.N. Shivraj (Madras) was elected as its president and P.N. Rajbhoj (Pune) as its General Secretary.[59]

Dr Babasaheb Ambedkar had got the unique opportunity of being appointed as Labour Member in the viceroy's Executive Council[60] with effect from 27, 1942. He continued as Labour member till 1946. During these days, he rose to the height of popularity and contributed substantially to the uplift of the Scheduled Castes and the Labourers. However, the caste Hindus in general went against him. Therefore, no candidate of his SCF could get elected in the general elections held for the provincial Assemblies in 1945.

In order to spread higher education among the Scheduled Castes in particular, among others, he founded Peoples Education Society at Bombay on 8, 1945. On behalf of the society he started Siddharth College of Arts and Science, (1946), Siddharth Night School (1947) Siddharth College of Commerce and Economics (1953), Siddharth College of Law (1956) all at Bombay and Milind Mahavidyalaya (1950), and Milind Multipurpose High School, (1955) at Aurangabad.

According to the Cabinet Mission Plan the elections to the Constituent Assembly of India were to be held in July 1946. However, Babasaheb Ambedkar had no hope to get elected from Bombay Legislature. Hence, he got elected to the Constituent Assembly from the Bengal Legislature, on July 19, 1946, with the help of his leutenant J.N. Mandal and the Muslim League Members. However, due to proposed partition of Bengal in 1947, he lost his membership which he got with great efforts. After having come to know the intellectual capacity, legal knowledge and staunch nationalism of Dr Babasaheb Ambedkar till then, the Congress nominated him from Bombay Legislature and got him elected to the Constituent Assembly, on July 23, 1947.

He got another unique opportunity of being nominated as the first Law Minister of free India in the Cabinet of Pandit Jawaharlal Nehru. Further, he was elected as Chairman of the Drafting Committee of the Constituent Assembly[61], on August 29, 1947. He drafted the Constitution and presented it to the Constituent Assembly on November 26, 1949 for its acceptance. The same Constitution, after having accepted with certain modifications by the Constituent Assembly, came into implementation on January 26, 1950.

Due to differences of opinion with Pandit Nehru on certain issues like Hindu Code Bill, Constitutional safeguards to the other Backward Classes foreign policy etc., he submitted resignation of his post on September 28, 1951 which came into effect on October 10, 1951.

In the general elections held in January 1952, he contested for Lok Sabha from Bombay (North) parliamentary constituency. N.S. Kajrolkar (Congress) was his opponent. Babasaheb Ambedkar was defeated in the election. Again he contested from Bhandara Parliamentary constituency (reserved-double member) in the by-election held in 1954. This time Nama Arjun Borkar (Congress) was his opponent. This time also Babasaheb Ambedkar was defeated and his opponent got elected. In the meantime, he was elected to the Rajya Sabha from the Bombay Legislature in March 1952. He was member of Rajya Sabha till the end of his life.

In 1953, he advised his followers in Marathwada region to launch a massive *satyagraha* for getting waste land for agricultural purpose.[62] Therefore, thousands of his followers launched *satyagraha* in which 1700 people courted arrest. However, he withdrew the *satyagraha* in November 1953.

It became clear by the end of April 1950 that he was inclined towards Buddhism. Therefore, he was invited as a delegate to the world Buddhist conference held at

Colombo, Sri Lanka on May 25, 1950. He participated in it. He participated in the World Buddhist Conference held at Rangoon (Burma) in December 1954. He founded Boudha Maha Sabha in 1955. He almost completed the writing of the Buddha and His Dhamma by the end of February, 1956. Ultimately, Babasaheb Ambedkar embracad Buddihism alongwith his family members on October 14, 1956 at Nagpur. Rev. Bhikku Chandramani of Kushinara officiated at the ceremony. Soon after that, Babasaheb Ambedkar himself gave Buddhism to his millions of followers came from several parts of the country. On October 16, 1956, he gave *Deeksha* of Buddhism to his followers at Chandrapur.

He went to Kathmandu (Nepal) to participate in the World Buddhist Conference held on November, 15 and 16, 1956 and returned to New Delhi on Nov.30, 1956.

He breathed his last on December 6, 1956 at his residence at 26, Alipore Road, New Delhi. The next day his body was put on funeral pyre at Dadar crematorium, Bombay.

"Ambedkar was a thick-set man with an oval face having a fierce air round it and a bald dome. He was five feet seven inches tall and weighed about one hundred and eighty pounds."[62(a)]

Babasaheb Ambedkar got a very a noble hearted and loving wife in Ramabai. She had to share utmost poverty in her early family life. Babasaheb Ambedkar was all the while busy with either reading and writing or solving the problems of the society. He could not spare sufficient time for family pleasure. During the gloomy days of Poona pact, she was very worried about safety of her husbad. In the words of Keer, "His wife was ill. During the past ten years he could not spare time to look after the members of his family. Whenever he could get some respite he looked into his home affairs. He had once taken his wife for a change of air to Dharwar; but there was not much improvement. The result was that though he was blessed with a good dutiful and pious wife, there was not much happiness."[62(b)]

As Karl Marx got a forever helping friend in Engels, Dr. Babasaheb Ambedkar also got a very co-operative friend in Naval Bhatena. When Babasaheb Ambedkar went to Colombia University in America in 1913, he had to live in poor condition in New York. During those days he happened to meet Naval Bhatena at Livingstone Hall Dormitory and stayed along with him and other Indian students. Naval Bhatena was a Parsi student lived with equal status without any caste discrimination. When Babasaheb was leaving for London in 1920 for his studies in Law and Economics, he incurred a loan of Rs five thousand from his friend Naval Bhatena. When he had no money to obtain a Sanad for starting his legal practice he had to seek financial co-operation from Naval Bhatena. While acknowledging the help of his friend, Babasaheb writes, "Believe me, I extremely regret to see you bothered on my account. I fully realise that the worries which I have thrown on you are more than even the thickest friend can bear. I only hope that my constant asking for something or other does not break your back and alienate you from me the only and dear friend of mine."[62(c)]

However, in his social and educational life Maharaja Sayajirao Gaikwad of Baroda and Chhatrapati Shahu Maharaj of Kolhapur helped him a lot.

[A] INFLUENCES AND INSPIRATIONS

Dr. Babasaheb Ambedkar was, however deeply influenced by three great preceptors namely Lord Buddha, Mahatma Kabir and Mahatma Phule. He himself said in unequivocal terms that, "I owe to three preceptors. Every one owes to his preceptor. I too. Their valuable teaching has however helped me in building my personality."[63]

All the three persons were really great personalities worthy to be called preceptors. Who is a great man ? He thinks that apart from being sincere and intellectual a Ma great man must be motivated by the dynamics of a "social purpose and must act as the scourge and the scavenger of society."[64] The preceptors whom he refers to with admiration and adoration apparently fulfil the tests of a great man.

[1] *Siddharth Goutam Buddha (B.C. 563 to B.C. 483) :*

Dr. Babasaheb Ambedkar was attracted to Buddha and his philosophy from his childhood itself. When young Bhim passed his matriculation in 1907, his community celebrated that event of unknown achievement for an 'untouchable'. On that occasion Krishnaji Arjun Keluskar, a teacher, social reformer and author presented him with a copy of his book, "Life of Goutam Buddha".[65] This book had an indelible impact on the mind of young Bhimrao.

When Goutama was at his prime age, there occured a dispute between his Sakya and the neighbouring Koliya kingdom on the distribution of water of river Rohini. The Sakya Sangh felt that the issue could be settled only by waging war against the Koliyas. Goutama differed the Sangha. He thought that, "it will sow the seeds of another war." However, the Sangha was adameant over its decision. Goutama had no alterative but to become a *Parivrajaka* and leave the Kingdom and thought to find the real remedy on the conflict of any kind being faced by human beings. He started his journey in search of a new light. He, however attained enlightenment under the Bodhi tree near Gaya, in the present Bihar State. He gave his first sermon to five *Parivrajakas* at Saranath. Subsequently, he continued teaching Dhamma to the people through out his life.

Buddha preached five precepts *(Panch Shila)* Eight-fold Path *(Arya Ashtangik Marg)* and ten virtues *(Das Paramitas)*. The Buddha revealed that there is suffering, all sufferings are caused by some cause, suffering can be removed and there is a way to remove the suffering. Here suffering is a wider term including every kind of suffering. These four noble truths instil in man an optimism to overcome his sufferings by the strict observance of Dhamma.

Dhamma means purity of body, purity of speech and purity of mind. Dhamma means practising self-control over passions so as to overcome all vices. Dhamma believes in the Doctrine of impermanence or perpetual changes occuring at every moment in the phenomenal world. Dhamma means belief in *Karma* as an instrument of moral order. "It is the *Kamma Niyam* and not God which maintains the moral order in the universe."[66] Thus, Dhamma means righteousness, which could be cultivated by *Pradnya, Karuna,Shila* and *Maitri*. Buddha had no faith in inequality-based on caste, creed or sex. He believed that worth and not birth is the measure of man. He preached liberty, equality and fraternity. Buddhism is not a religion in the tranditional sense of the term. It is but a way of life.

Buddha was a great rationalist. He said very categorically that, "accept not on hearsay nor by tradition, nor by what people say accept not because it is in the scriptures, by mere logic, nor by inference, nor by consideration of appearances, nor because it accords with your view, nor because you think it must be right, nor out of respect, with the thought that "one must revere a recluse."[67] He should accept that which is good to him and to the humanity at large.

Therefore, Dr. Babasaheb Ambedkar embraced Buddhism on 14th October, 1956 on *Vijaya Dashami* Day, at Nagpur and gave it to his millions of followers for enriching knowledge and wisdom. He, of course studied Buddhism in its true perspective and wrote *'Buddha and His Dhamma'* for its proper comprehension.

[2] *Mahatma Kabir* (1398 to 1494):

Dr. Babasaheb Ambedkar himself said that, "My second

preceptor is Kabir. My father belonged to Kabir Panth. Therefore, I am greatly influenced by the personality and philosophy of Kabir."[68] Subhedar Ramji Sakapal, the father of Babasaheb Ambedkar had embraced Kabir Panth in 1896, and strictly followed it.

Saint Kabir believed in human equality. He did not believe in Varna, Caste, untouchability and superstitions. He was a staunch propounder of communal harmony and Hindu-Muslim Unity. He composed many thought provoking poems or songs, which are comprised in *'Kabir Bijak'*.

Kabir did not believe in any God as such. His God is but *'Nirgun Brahma'*, which was without any attributes. It is thus simply a 'cause' behind some 'effect'. He preached rationality and morality throughout his life.

[3] *Mahatma Jyotiba Phule* : (1827 to 1890)

Mahatma Phule was a great social revolutionary thinker and an active crusader against all the social evils. He believed in social equality. He thought that "the creator of all is one." All the human beings, irrespective of their caste, sex and place of birth are socially equal. He said that the Vedas, which created differences among the human beings are false.

Saint Kabir rightly thought that the Shudras and untouchables had to suffer only due to their imposed 'Ignorance' or 'Avidya'.[69] He emphasised on removing illiteracy and ignorance. Therefore, he started in Pune the first ever school in India especially for the untouchables in 1848. He started many other schools in the vicinity of Pune for the children of the shurdas and untouchables. In his missionary work, his saintly wife Savitribai Phule gave utmost co-operation to him.

Mahatma Phule was against all sorts of exploitation. He was a true sympathiser of the peasants and workers. In his *"Shetkayancha Asud"* he stated that the *Bhat-Brahmins* squeez money on some superstitions and fictitious pretext.

Eventually, Mahatma Phule founded a new socio-religious movement known as *"Sarvajanik Satyadharma"* in 1873 for preaching and propagating his thoughts and organising the exploited people under one banner.[70]

In addition to the above said three preceptors Dr Babasaheb Ambedkar owes to a great extent to other thinkers. They are:

[4] *Subhedar Ramji Maloji Sakpal* (1848-1913) :

Subhedar Ramji Sakpal, father of Babasaheb Ambedkar was a Subedar Major in British Indian Army. After retirement from the service, he came to Depoli, Ratnagiri in Maharashtra in 1894 and got employed as store-keeper. In 1896 he was transferred to Satara. He shifted to Mumbai in 1904 for the purpose of educating his children in good school and lived at Dabak Chawl in Parel area.

Ramji Subedar was staunch follower of *Kabirpanth*. He used to sing the Abhanga and Padas of Saint Chokha Mela, Tukaram Maharaj and Mahatma Kabir. He used to maintain peace, cleanliness and standard in his house.[71]

He gave high moral and cultural education to his son Bhimrao and inspired him to take higher education and serve the community in a better way.

[5] *John Dewey* (1859-1952):

John Dewey was a propounder of the theory of Instrumentalism. He thought that the object of philosophy is not merely to speculate but to solve problems of the needy people, such as solving bad sanitation, poor working conditions disparity in distribution of income and distribution of material and cultural values produced by the technological revolution.

John Dewey was a realist. He was more concerned with the examination of how government actually works. People actually want satisfaction and to avoid pain rather than ideas and ideals.

In his view society is pluralistic, as such the state was merely one of those institutions or associations. "The worship of constitutional law was wrong, the life of the law has not been logic; it has been experience."[72]

[6] *J.S. Mill* (1806-1873):

The famous British political thinker James Stuart Mill is known as a protagonist of human liberty. He thought that every person must have liberty to think, liberty to express and liberty to act accordingly. No state or religion should restrain the liberty of an individual. Individual should have full and unrestrained liberty to develop his own personality. However, liberty of one should not be an obstacle in the way of others. Mill divides all actions into two: self-regarding and other regarding. So far as self-regarding actions are concerned, he has absolute freedom, whereas in respect of other regarding actions he is amenable to the society.[73]

Mill was a man of letters. He became editor of *"London Review"*. In 1856, Mill became the chief of the office of Indian correspondence in the office of East India Company, in London. He retired from his company service in 1858. During 1866 to 1868 he was a member of Parliament.

[7] *Thomas Jafferson* (1743-1826) :

Jafferson had actively participated in the war of independence fought against the British colonialism. He participated in the second conference of the Americans held at Philadelphia in 1776. He drafted the Declaration of independence made at that time. He was elected as President of USA in 1800, and again in 1804.

Dr. Babasaheb Ambedkar was greatly influenced by the provisions of the fundamental rights included in the famous declaration of independence. He referred to the declaration of independence in his speech with great respect in the Pacific Relation Conference held in

Quebeck (Canada) in December 1942. It was categorically stated in the said declaration that people got the natural right to revolt against that government which rules irresponsibly.

Jefferson a constitutional philospher said that the Constitution ought to be amendable according to exigencies of time. Dr. Babasaheb referred to Jefferson's opinion in his speech delivered in the Constituent Assembly on 25th November 1949. He said that, "we may consider each generation as distinct nation, with a right, by the will of the majority, to bind themselves, but none to bind the succeeding generation, more than the inhabitants of another country."[74] This amply reflects as to how much he was influenced by the Constitutional thought of Jafferson.

[A] HIS WRITINGS:

Dr. Babasaheb Ambedkar was a prolific writer. He had written many books: They are as under.

1.	Castes in India	1917
2.	The Problem of the Rupee	1923
3.	The Evolution of Provincial Finance in British India.	1925
4.	Annihilation of Caste	1936
5.	Federation versus Freedom	1939
6.	Pakistan or the Partition of India	1940
7.	Mr. Gandhi and the Emancipation of the Untouchables.	1942
8.	Ranade, Gandhi and Jinnah	1943
9.	What Congress and Gandhi have done to the Untouchables.	1945
10.	Communal deadlock and a way to solve it.	1945
11.	Who were the Shudras ?	1946

12.	States and Minorities. What are their rights and how to secure them in the Constitution of free India.	1947
13.	The Untouchables who were they and why they became untouchables?	1948
14.	Maharashtra as a Linguistic Province	1948
15.	Thoughts on Linguistic States	1955
16.	The Buddha and His Dhamma	1957 (Posthumously)
17.	Philosophy of Hinduism	1987 (Posthumously)
18.	Riddles in Hinduism.	1987 (Posthumously)
19.	Untouchables or the Children of of India's Ghetto	1989 (Posthumously)
20.	Pali English Dictionary	1998 (Posthumously)

Ambedkar's whole life was a mission aimed at the emancipation of the Depressed Classes from untouchability, casteism, ignorance, irreligion, poverty and exploitation. Though he was misunderstood by some people, he was a true nationalist, humanist and rationalist of his times. He, however rendered invaluable services to the nation as a whole. Therefore, the Government of India, honoured him (posthumously)[75] With the nation's highest civilian award, *"Bharat Ratna"* on April 14, 1990 and declared the year 1990-91, being his birth centenary year, as the year of Social Justice.

Conclusion

The life and mission of the two great men of the world could be described as a unique saga in the emancipatory struggle of the persecuted humanity. It, however reflects certain instances experiences and confrontations of their individual life which are more or less similar. Both of them have left the rich legacy of knowledge and sacrifice for noble cause.

References and Notes

1. Mehring Franz : Karl Marx : *The story of his life*: p. 3. George Allen and Unwin Ltd. 40, Musem Street, London (1948)
2. Volkov Genrikh: *Birth of A Genious.* The Development of the Personality and World Outlook of Karl Marx: p. 33. Progress Publishers, Moscow (1978).
3. Mehring Franz : Karl Marx : p. 27, 28.
4. Stepanova E.: Short Biography of Karl Marx: p. 10. Progrees Publishers, Moscow (4th Edn.1968)
5. *Ibid.,* p.10
6. Volkov Genrikh: Birth of a Genius. p. 38.
7. *Ibid.,* p. 39.
8. Mehring Franz: Karl Marx. p.6.
9. Volkov Genrikh: birth of a genius. p. 45.
10. *Ibid.,* p. 179.
11. *Ibid.,* p. 182.
12. *Ibid.,* p. 182.
13. Stepanova E. Short Biography of Karl Marx. p. 63
14. Volkov Genrikh: Birth of a Genius. p. 195.
15. Ibid., p. 195.
16. Ibid., p. 196.
17. Ott Ruhle: Karl Marx: *His Life and Work*, pp. 202-203 (1929) Quated by S.C. Pant-Western pol. theory. p. 218
18. Patil Vishwas : *Karl Marx Vyakti Ani Vichar.* (Marathi) p. 45 Padma Gandha Prakashan, Pune.
19. Mehring Franz: Karl Marx : The Story of his life. p. 172.
20. Volkov Genrikh: *Birth of a Genius.* p. 62
21. Stepanova E. Short Biography of Karl Marx p. 14. Progress Publishers, Moscow p. 14. (4th Edition 1968).
22. *Ibid.,* p. 35
23. *Ibid.,* p. 39
24. *Ibid.,* p. 49

25. Yuvi Sdobnikov. Karl Marx: A Biography. p. 264. Progress Publishers, Moscow.1973.
25a. Lenin : Collected Works : Vol. 21. p. 48.
25b. Stepanova: Short Biography p. 77.
26. Volkov Generikh. p. 186.
27. Johnson Gerald W.Communism: A Study of Revolution. p. 3.
Bantam Books, New York. (1966)
28. For details see History of Economic thought by H.L. Bhatia. pp. 69-110
Vikas Publishing House, Jangpura, New Delhi. (1978).
29. Volkov Genrikh : Birth of a Genius. p. 22.
30. Bhatia H.L. History of Economic Thought p. 265.
31. Ibid., p. 222.
32. Volkov Genrikh: Birth of a Genius. p. 55.
33. *Ibid.,* p.58
34. Yuri Sdobnikov. Karl Marx: p. 32.
35. See for details: *A History of Political Theory by George H. Sabine.* pp. 520-668.
36. Bhatia H.L. History of Economic Thought. p. 263.
37. Misra B. Capitalism, Socialism and Planning. p. 19. Oxford & IBH Publishing Co. New Delhi. (Edn.1982).
38. *Ibid.,* p. 22
39. Karl Marx: *Manifesto of The Communist Party.* p. 92. People's Publishing House (P) Ltd., New Delhi (2012)
40. Volkov Genrikh : Birth of a Genius. p. 195.
41. Indore was a Princely State. There was a military camp of the British Government in India at Mhow.
42. The biographer of Babasaheb Ambedkar C.B. Khairmade States the surname of the Leader as 'Sankpal', (Vol. I. p. 6) though it has been stated as 'Sakpal' by other authors. The name 'Sankpal' seems to be the spoilt of 'Sanghpal', which means the protector of the Sangh or the Buddhist Sangh. According to the Broken Men theory given by Babasaheb Ambedkar in his *"The Untouchables"* (1948): The untouchables were Buddhists in the long past. Probably, the ancestors of Babasaheb Ambedkar, who were presumably Buddhists might have tried to protect the Buddhist Sangha from their harassment by the opponents of Buddhism. Hence, the honorific name-Sanghpal-might have been given to his family.

43. During his college days at Bombay, he used to get a scholarship of Rs 25 per month from his benefactor Maharaja Sayajirao Gaikwad of Baroda State.
43a. Again the Maharaja of Baroda sanctioned pound 11 1/2 scholarship per month.
44. Keer Dhanajaya : Dr. Ambedkar: Life and Mission. p. 26 Popular Prakashan, Tardeo Rd, Bombay. (Edn.1971)
45. For details see, Evidence before the Southborough Committee, given on 27th January 1919, in Dr. Babasaheb Ambedkar writings and speeches, Vol.1.
Education Department, Government of Maharashtra, 1979.
46. The Official editor of *Mook Naik* was P.N. Bhatkar but later on, when Babasaheb was in England for higher studies, D.N. Gholap became its editor.
47. For details see 'Vidarbhatil Chalvalicha itihas' written by H.L. Kosare. pp. 49-62.
Gyan Pradip Prakashan, Navishukravari, Nagpur, (1984)
48. For details see 'Dr. Bhimrao Ramji Ambedkar Charitra : Second Volume by Changdeo Bhavanrao Khairmode, (pp. 106-143).
Boudhajan Panchayat Samiti, Parel, Mumbai (1958).
49. For details see 'Dr. Ambedkar: *Life and Mission'* by Dhananjay Keer. pp.70-80, 97-107.
50. Its editor was Babasaheb Ambedkar himself.
51. For details see Vol. 2 of DBAWS (1982).
52. Keer Dhananjay: Dr. Ambedkar : Life and Mission. p. 124.
53. Ibid., p. 137
54. For details see *Vidarbhatil Dalit Chalvalicha itihas*, by H.L. Kosare (1984) pp. 147-149.
55. *Ibid.*, pp.185-193.
56. For details see DBAWS Vol. 2 (1982).
57. Its first editor was Deorao Naik. From 1932 to 39 B.R. Kadrekar edited it. Then for sometime G. N. Sahastrabuddhe, then R.D. Bhandare and then B.C. Kamble edited it. From 1950 onwards Y.B. Ambedkar edited it.
58. Keer Dhananjay: Dr. Ambedkar: Life and Mission. p. 313 (1971).
59. For details see, Political thought of Dr. Babasaheb Ambedkar by Dr. R.K. Kshirsagar. pp. 98-107.
Intellectual Publishing House Daryaganj, Ansari Road, New Delhi. (1992)
60. That time Lord Linlithgo was Viceroy of India.

61. Other members of the Drafting Committee were: Alladi Krishanaswami Ayyar. N. Gopalswami Ayyangar, K.M. Munshi, Muhammad Sadulla, B.L. Mitter and D.P. Khaitan. Subsequently N. Madhav Rau and T.T. Krishnamachari were respectively taken in place of B.L. Mitter and D.P. Khaitan.
62. Keer Dhananjay: Dr. Ambedkar : Life and Mission. p. 451.
62a. *Ibid.,* p. 467.
62b. *Ibid.,* p. 62.
62c. *Ibid.,* p. 46.
63. Ganjare M.F. (Ed.) Dr. Babasaheb Ambedkaranchi Bhashane. Vol. 61. p. 99.
Ashok Prakashan, Prabuddha Nagar, Nagpur (1976).
64. DBAWS: Vol. 1. p. 215.
65. Keer Dhananjay: Dr. Ambedkar: Life and Mission. p. 20. Popular Prakashan, Bombay (3rd Edn. 1971)
66. DBAWS: p. 243. (1992) Vol. I
67. Ibid., p. 485.
68. Ganjare M.F. (Ed.) *Dr. Babasaheb Ambedkarachi Bhashane.* Vol. VI. p.100. (1976)
69. Phule said "For want of education intellect deteriorated, for want of intellect morality decayed, for want of morality progress stopped, for want of Progress Wealth Vanished, for want of Wealth the Shudras Perished. All these sorrows sprang from illiteracy."
70. For details see his book, *'Sarvajanik Satya Dharma Pustak',* in 'Mahatma Phule, Samagra Vangmay". Edited by Dhananjay Keer and S.G. Malshe. Maharashtra Rajya Sahitye ani Sanskriti Mandal, Mumbai (Second Edn.1980)
71. Khairmode Changdeo Bhavanrao: Dr. Bhimrao Ramji Ambedkar (Vol. I). Pratap Prakashan, Giergaon, Mumbai. (2nd Edn.1968).
72. Sharma R.P. Modern Western Political Thought. p. 225. Sterling Publishers Pvt. Ltd. New Delhi. (4th Edn.1976).
73. Mill J.S. Utilitarianism, on Liberty p. 135. Colins Press, London. (1962).
74. DBAWS.Vol.13. p. 1211.
75. His second wife 'Maisaheb' (Sharada aliyas) Savita Ambedkar received the award from President R.Venkataraman in a Special Ceremony at Rashtrapati Bhavan, New Delhi on April 14, 1990.

3

Basic Doctrines

While studying the thoughts of any philosophers it becomes inevitable to take into account certain basic concepts or doctrines. They provide the premises on which the thoughts are based. So far as the philosophy of Karl Marx and Babasaheb Ambedkar is concerned there are certain basic doctrines, which we need to comprehend properly so that we may be able to appreciate their philosophy.

[A]

(1) *Dialectical Materialism*:

According to Genrikh Volkov, "The very term dialectics was born in Ancient Greece and meant the art of conducting a dispute, or dialogue, the art of manoeuvring your fellow-conversationalist into an impasse, of making him finally state something which was the direct opposite of what he had asserted at the beginning. With time the term dialectics acquired a somewhat different sense. It began to mean the fluidity, the contradictory character of the actual processes of nature, society and thought, and the development from the simple to the complex by means of the unity and clash of opposites. The first Greek philosophers, Heraclitus, Anaxagoras, Parmenides, Zeno Democritus, Socretes, and Plato, were skilled dialecticians. It was they who turned *dialectics* into a consciously applied method of thinking, of cognising the world around. The Ancient Greek philosophers give an integrated picture of the universe, intuitively grasping in the most important and universal causal relations. Greek philosophy bequeathed to us a developed, dialectically flexible system of concepts and categories which is still used successfully to explain and interpret the World."[1]

Dialeticism is a process which attempts to find out the absolute Truth. "The dialectical process is thus one of thesis, anti-thesis and synthesis. The thesis affirms a proposition. The anti-thesis denies or in Hegelian Terminology 'negates' it. The synthesis embraces what is true in both the thesis and the anti-thesis and thus brings us one step nearer to reality."[2]

Hegel has developed the dialectic philosophy for the explanation of social phenomenon. According to Hegel, 'every thought or concept is relative, not absolute',. Only idea or spirit is absolute. The state is the reflex of that absolute idea or ultimate reality. Every idea before reaching to that stage has to pass through the dialectical process as distinguished from mechanical process. In the dialectic process every idea is born out of other, and it is subjected to criticism. It becomes anti-thesis. The thesis and anti-thesis lead to synthesis. After the passage of sometime the synthesis forms thesis, thesis is criticised which finally gives rise to synthesis. Thus, the process of dialeticism is in continuation forever.

Karl Marx accepted the dialecticism given by Hegel, but applied it to his theory of *materialism*. He, however replaced 'idea' or thought with materialism. According to Random House dictionary, *"Materialism"* means "philosophical theory that regards matter and its motions as constituting the universe, and all phenomena including those of mind, as due to material agencies." Marx thought that the world develops in accordance with the laws of movement in matter. The spiritual life is merely a reflection of the matter. "Marx conceived of man as an economic rather than a political animal."[3] He is an idol of all instincts and passion. From this class-struggle comes into existence. There will be logical end of class-struggle with the proletariat revolution and withering away of the state.

Volkov states that, "The dialectical method still has to show what it is capable of in scientific cognition. The natural sciences feel a compelling need to generalise, to put the accumulated material in order, to process it dialectically, to integrate the unco-ordinated achievements of the sciences on the different flanks with the help of a new conceptual and methodological apparatus.

This is where natural science enters the higher spheres of theoretical thought. It is inevitably faced with the task of organising all the results achieved into a definite system, of expounding them within the framework of a single theory. We already find such a task on the agenda of modern physics, biology and ecology. There is no other way of solving it apart from the method of ascendancy from the abstract to the concrete.

The dialecto-materialist method is a powerful weapon in the hands of the researcher. It helps him to choose a correct path-finder, not to lose his bearings, not to stray into an impasse. It helps him to see the problem in places where experiment and mathematical analysis cannot yet discover it. Yet all this is subject to the condition that the researcher does not simply know the philosophical tenets, but has mastered this method to perfection."[4].

According to D.D. Kosambi, "Dialectical materialism holds that matter is primeval, and the properties of matter are inexhaustible. Mind is an aspect of matter, being a function of the brain. Ideas, therefore, are not primary phenomena, but rather the reflection of material processes and changes upon human consciousness which is itself a material process."[5]

(2) *Materialistic Interpretation of History*

Karl Marx wanted to discover the law and method of historical and social change. His inquisitive mind took him to his predecessor and a great thinker Hegel.

Karl Marx found in Hegel's philosophy the way to interpret history in the light of Hegelian view of 'ideas'. Hegel thought the basic principle behind any change in the society was the idea. Ideas move the man, inspire the man to act and give a new turn to the society. However, the ideas exist, move and act according to dialectical way. Ideas are developed by criticism of the ideas and ultimately they come to the conclusion in the form of synthesis. In the course of history, the synthesis also turns into thesis and the same process continues. Thus, any event, any change or any phenomenon comes into existence only because of some 'idea'.

Karl Marx thought that the dialectical method of inquiry would lead any investigator to truth. Therefore, he applied Hegelian ideas to the human affairs. He however found that it is not the 'idea' or 'spirit' behind the history, but the 'matter' or economic factors are behind the history. Hegel viewed history as the self-realisation of the 'absolute idea'. On the contrary, Marx thought that it is not the abstract or intangible ideas, but the material forces play the important role in the development of human history. In the words of Karl Marx, "In the social production which men carry on they enter into definite relations that are indispensable and independent of their will. These relations of production correspond to a definite stage of development of their material forces of production. The sum total of these relations of production constitutes the economic structure of society, the real foundation on which rise legal and political superstructures, and to which correspond definite forms of social consciousness. The mode of production in material life determines the general character of the social, political and spiritual process of life. It is not the consciousness of men that determines their existence, but on the contrary, their social existence determines their consciousness. At a certain stage of their development, the material forces of production in society come in conflict with the existing relations of productions, or what is but a legal expression for the same thing with the property relations within which they had been at work before. From forms of development of the forces of production these relations turn into their fetters. Then comes the period of social revolution. With the change of the economic foundation the entire immense superstructure is more or less rapidly transformed."[6] Thus, the means of production that ultimately determine all the political, legal, cultural and religious institutions and beliefs. Mind and spirit are the products of matter. However, Marx ignores the part played by non-economic forces, like religion, nationalism and ideological attachment.

He said very categorically that "social relations are closely bound up with productive forces. In acquiring new productive forces men change their mode of production; and in changing their mode of production, in changing the way of earning, their living, they change their social relations. The hand Mill gives you society with the feudal lord; the steam Mill, society with the industrial capitalist."[7]

(3) *Economic Determinism*

Karl Marx contemplates that any system of production carries with it a corresponding way of distributing the social product. The way of distribution creates a structure of social classes. "Its mode of production at any given time explains its political and indeed its whole cultural condition at that time and changes in the system of production explain the corresponding changes that occur in its politics and culture. This in bare outline is Marx's theory of economic determinism."[8]

The structure of classes that exists in a society at any given period is itself an historical product which changes with the forces of economic production. The religion, morality and corresponding forms of consciousness forms 'Superstructure' depending on 'economic base'.

Accordingly, the material condition, is not determined by consciousness but material conditions determine consciousness.

The material conditions are important, as they determine the position and status of the individual in the society. The Proletarian Class in England or Germany was underpaid. Hence, they were compelled to live in drudgery.

Economic determinism implies that it is not the divine power, but the economic factors which determine the economic status of the human beings. It may change according to change in time and change in the mode of production.

(4) *Theory of Surplus Value*

The theory of surplus value forms a pivotal part in the philosophy of scientific socialism developed by Karl Marx. In this process, he defined a commodity. Accordingly, "A Commodity is in the first place, an object outside us, a thing that by its properties satisfies human wants of some sort or another."[9] Every commodity or thing has utility value. It is an assemblage of many properties, as such it is of use in various ways. Thus, every commodity has: (1) Use Value; and (2) Exchange Value.

"The utility of a thing makes it a Use-value."[10] "Exchange-value, at first sight, presents itself as a quantitative relation, as the proportion in which values in use of one sort are exchanged for those of another sort, a relation constantly changing with time and place."[11] The commodities are exchanged in the proportions in which they are exchangeable, whatever those proportions may be, can always be represented by an equation, between the two. The magnitude of this value is to be measured by the quantity of the labour contained in the article.

"A thing can be a use-value without having value. This is the case whenever its utility to man is not due to labour. Such are air, virgin soil, natural meadows etc. A thing can be useful, and the product of human labour, without being a commodity. Whoever directly satisfies his wants with the product of his own labour, creates, indeed, use values, but not commodities. Lastly, nothing can have value without being an object of utility."[12] Thus, the use values or products are combinations of two elements matter and labour. They are exchanged for a certain value. Money "serves as Universal measure of value".[13] In the words of Marx, "The commodity that functions as a mreasure of value, and, either in its own person or by a representative, as the medium of circulation, is money."[14]

Where the means of production are privately owned, the labour has to be purchased equivalent to the exchange value of the labour power. "The capitalist buys labour power in order to use it."[15] Thus, the capitalist becomes owner of the labour power, and the labourer works under the control of the capitalist. He, however desires to produce a commodity whose value shall be higher than the sum of the values of the components used in its production. His aim is to produce not only use value but surplus value.

"If we now compare the two processes of producing value and of creating surplus value, we see that the latter is nothing but the continuation of the former beyond a definite point. If on the one hand, the process be not carried beyond the point, where the value paid by the capitalist for the labour power is replaced by an exact equivalent, it is simply a process of producing value, if, on the other hand, it be continued beyond that, it becomes a process of creating surplus value."[16]

"The capital 'C' is made up of two components,' one, the sum of money 'C' utilised on the means of production and the other sum of money 'V' expended upon the labour power; 'C' represents the portion that has become constant capital, and 'V' the portion that has become variable capital. At first then, *C = C+V;* if $500 is the capital advanced, its components may be such that the $500 = $ 410 const. + $ 90 var. When the process of production is finished, we get commodity whose value = *(C+V) + S,* where 'S' is the surplus value; or taking former figures, the value of this commodity may be ($ 410 Const. + $90 Var) + $ 90 surpl. The original capital has now changed from 'C to C', from $500 to $590. The difference is 'S' or a surplus value of $90."[17]

Thus 'surplus-value is the difference between the value of the product and the value of the elements consumed in the formation of that product; in other words, of the means of production and the labour power.'

There are two ways in which the capitalist can think of increasing the surplus value per worker. One is to lengthen the working day, and the other is to shorten the portion of the working day which goes to provide the subsistence (or payment for the labour power) by increasing the productiveness of labour. "By increase in the productiveness of labour, we mean, generally, an alteration in the labour process, of such a kind as to shorten the labour-time socially necessary for the production of a commodity and to endow a given quantity of labour with the power of producing a greater quantity of use-value."[18]

Karl Marx explains the Absolute surplus value and relative surplus value. In his words, "The surplus-value produced by prolongation of the working day, I call absolute surplus value. On the other hand, the surplus value arising from the curtailment of the necessary labour-time and from the corresponding alteration in the respective lengths of the two components of the working day. I call relative surplus-value."[19]

He, however thinks that the surplus value is exclusively appropriated by the capitalists. This facilitates accumulation of capital which is further used to augmenting the production. Thus, the capitalist becomes rich and rich whereas the labourer due to his exploitation becomes poor and poor. This further causes for difference and distinction between the two classes.

[B]

(1) *Dialectical Realism*

According to Hegel, "mind or idea was primary and real and matter a product thereof. Marx held matter to be primary and mind to be its highest development."[20] According to Buddha, "matter and mind are inter-dependent. There is no primary or secondary substance. Indeed there is no substance at all. Every substance is a process a process of coming into being and passing away. Here we find in the same breath a high form of dialectics, and at the same time a rejection of the materialistic doctrine."[21]

Buddha's approach towards all the problems and phenomenon was rationalistic, dialectic and realistic. In the words of Y. Balrammoorty he was, "The first Indian thinker who made dialectics, the law of eternal change, the central core of his philosophy. Buddhist philosophy arose in the course of an idealogical struggle against the existing upanishadic philosophy, which by that time became completely rigid and metaphysical."[22] On this background Buddha advanced the doctrine of 'Dependent Origination' to explain the cause of origination of any phenomenon.

He had, of course no faith in the existence of God; heaven or hell. It is only here to get the results of all good or evil activities. Man is the centre of any thing. He himself is benefactor of his person.[23]

The law of dependent origination is the core of Buddhist philosophy. Dr. Babasaheb Ambedkar being a true follower of Buddhism had faith in this theory of dependent origination. It explains the origin of anything or object in terms of 'cause and effect.'

In his very first discourse at Saranath, the Buddha said that, "Let us put aside such unprofitable and unsolvable questions *(avya-ktani)* as the questions of beginning and end—nothing exists by itself, nothing is absolute. Everything depends on something else. Everything is the effect of some cause. As long as the cause exists effect also exists. When the cause ceases to be, the effect also vanishes. Everything is relative cause and effect are interrelated. One thing flows from the other."[24]

Allied to the concept of 'Dependent Origination' is the concept of impermanence. In other words, the concept of dependent origination implies or contemplates the concept of impermanence or change. Buddha was a non-eternalist thinker. The process of cause and effect is in continuation. "The effect then transforms itself into a cause and produces another effect. The transformation of cause into effect and *vice versa* is an endless process."[25]

Later on, Nagarjuna a great Buddhist philosopher explained the concept of Dependent Origination, in the form of theory of relativity. He said that, "nothing has its own being; everything is what it is in relation to other things and nothing has an independent existence. *"Bhavah Svantantro Nasti."* Moreover, nothing is an integral entity: things we see and deal with are made up of constituents *(dharmas)*. But even these ultimate constituents have no substantiality or self and neither endurance nor momentariness. All things are mutually dependent and related: This mutual dependence and interrelationship makes them what they are."[26]

According to Nagarjuna, "reality is relative and not absolute. Everything is real within certain limits. Beyond those limits it is unreal'. Is the objective world real? Yes, it is real as far as worldly knowledge goes *(Samvruti Satya)*.

But from the view of the transcendental "Truth *(Paramarth Satya)* it is unreal."[27] "The world is a flux, things are constantly changing, they are caused and are causing, they act and are being acted upon and they come into existence and cease to be."[28]

Following Buddha, Dr. Babasaheb Ambedkar states that, "a human being is always changing always growing. He is not the same at two different moments of his life." He further states that, "if things were not subject to continual change but were permanent and unchangeable, the evolution of all of life from one kind to the other, and the development of living things would come to a dead stop."[29] As Buddha said,—

"Nothing was infallible and nothing could be final. Everything must be open to re-examination and reconsideration whenever grounds for re-examination and reconsideration arise."

"Man must know the Truth and real truth. To him freedom of thought was the most essential thing. And he was sure that freedom of thought was the only way to the discovery of truth."[30]

In the words of Prof. Lakshmi Narasu, Buddha said that, "you shall free your mind of ignorance and be anxious to learn Truth, lest you fail prey to doubt...." Thou shouldst never wrangle about Dharma and then seek to have those doubts solved into which Thou mayest arrive. Let no doubts like these ever take possession of the mind.[31] Accordingly, Buddhism does not underestimate the value of doubt during the period of investigation".

The discovery of truth is possible only when there is freedom to think and express, freedom to accept or reject and freedom to examine and re-examine any fact or phenomenon. A researcher has to firstly presume that nothing is infallible and final and absolute. He has to "criticise" the thesis. From this anti-thesis he would go to synthesis or "real truth". The truth has to be examined with reference to time and space and come to conclusion. One should not take anything for granted. One should not accept anything because it is written in canonical literature or said by a great man or trickled down by tradition.

Dr. Babasaheb Ambedkar accepted this thought of Buddha and preached and acted upon this thought throughout his life. His *'dialectic'* was not only for historical facts or material facts, but also for any social, political, religious, scientific and cultural facts. His way of probing of knowledge was applicable to all the facts and phenomenon. It was a scientific and rational way of reaching to the 'Truth' in the real perspective.

(2) *Pluralistic Interpretation of History*

According to Dr. Babasaheb Ambedkar history is the creation of human beings. However, before coming to this conclusion, he takes a very cursory view of the opinions expressed by different thinkers in this respect. "There have been," he states, "three different views on the causes of historical changes. We have had the Augustinian theory of history, according to which history is only an unfolding of a divine plan in which mankind is to continue through war and suffering until that divine plan is completed at the day of judgement. There is the view of Buckle, who held that history was made by Geography and Physics. Karl Marx propounded a third view. According to him history was the result of economic forces. None of these three would admit that history is the biography of greatmen. Indeed they deny man any place in the making of history. No one except theologians accept the Augustinian theory of history. As to Buckle and Marx, while there is truth in what they say, their views do not represent the whole truth. They are quite wrong in holding that impersonal forces are everything and that man is no factor in the making of history. That impersonal forces are a determining factor can not be denied. But that the effect of impersonal forces depend on man must also be admitted. Flint may not exist everywhere. But where it does exist, it needs man to strike flint against flint to make fire."[32] He concludes that, "man therefore is a factor in the making of history and that environmental forces, whether impersonal or social if they are the first are not the last things."[33]

Dr. Babasaheb Ambedkar takes a very comprehensive view of the historical facts. He does not deny the role of social and material factors in making history, but he gives primordial importance to the role of man his ideas and deeds. History is but the reflex of the deeds of great men who are responsible for bringing about social, economic, political, cultural and scientific changes.

He gave more or less equal importance to the social factors in making the history. He said that, "history bears out the proposition that political revolutions have always been preceded by social and religious revolutions."[34] "The emancipation of the mind and the soul is a necessary preliminary for the political expansion of the people."[35]

The 'self-consciousness' has played a great role in Indian history. It is true that the self conscious untouchable soldiers under the British leadership brought down the hegemony of Brahmanism during Peshwa despotic rule at Koregaon in 1818. Even they gave a very valiant fight to al most all the despotic feudal lords in 1857, and brought them to dust at once. The role of self-conscious movement of the Depressed Classes continued till its logical conclusion in 1950, when India became a sovereisn democratic Republic. Thus history reveals the fact that from Manu to modern age religious ides of caste, untouchability and *Brahmanism* are at the base of historical development. Therefore, Dr. Babasaheb Ambedkar said that the struggle for supremacy between Buddhism and Brahmanism has "compeltely moulded the history of India."[36] His interpretation of history is however based on logic and reason.

While explaining as to how the primitive society became a settled community Dr. Babasaheb Ambedkar states that the primitive society was a nomadic society. "But it was, nomadic not because of any migratory instinct. Nor was it due to any mental trait Pecular to it. It was the result of the fact that the earliest form of the wealth held by primitive society was cattle. Primitive society was migratory because its wealth namely the cattle, was migratory. Cattle went after new pastures. Primitive society by reason of its love for cattle, therefore went whenever its cattle carried it. Primitive society became fixed in its abode in other words became a settled community, when a new species of wealth was discovered. This new species of wealth was land. This happened when primitive society learned the art of farming and cultivating land. Wealth became fixed at one place when it changed its form from cattle to land. With this change primitive society also became settled at the same place."[37]

The professions like involuntary servitude, devadasi or scavenging brought bad name and grinding poverty to the so-called untouchables. These professions determined their status. Therefore, Babasaheb Ambedkar exhorted his brethren to abandon such ugly professions. He advised them to adopt clean professions maintain high moral and cultural standard. Following Mahatma Phule, he propounded that, education brings consciousness, as such it is 'base' and all other things form 'Super-structure.'[38]

(3) *Social Determinism*

Dr. Babasaheb Ambedkar believing in Buddhism repudiated the theory of supernaturalism or divine theory of existence. There are various reasons as to why he rejected the doctrine of the existence of God. He states that nobody has seen God. Belief in God is based on mere speculation and creating superstitions. Having not seen the God, how can one believes in God. It is a case like man falling in love with a woman whom he has not seen. If God is good or moral, how he creates bad immoral and criminal progeny. If the God is omniscient and merciful, why does he not give happiness to all. Following the doctrine of *Patit Samutpada*, he asks the question "Did God create something out of nothing or did he create something out of something? It is impossible to believe that something could have been created out of nothing. If the socalled God has created something out of something, then that something out of which something new was created, has been in existence before he created anything. God cannot therefore be called the creator of that something which has existed before him. If something has been created by somebody out of something before God created anything then God can not be said to be the creator or the first cause."[39]

Dr. Babasaheb Ambedkar being a True follower of Buddha, states that, "a sentient being is a compound thing consisting of certain physical elements and certain mental elements". They are called *Khandas*—

The *Rupa Khanda* primarily consists of the physical elements such as earth, water, fire and air. They constitute the Body or *Rupa*.

Besides *Rupa Khanda* there is such a thing as *Nama Khanda* which goes to makeup a sentient being.

This *Nama Khanda* is called *Vinana*, or consciousness. This *Nama Khanda* includes the three mental elements: *Vedana* (sensation springing from contact of the six senses with the world) *Sanna* (perception); *Sankhara* (States of mind).

"How is consciousness produced?"

"What the Buddha said was that whereever there was *rupa or Kaya*, there was consciousness accompanying it".

"To give an analogy from science, there is an electric field and wherever there is an electric field it is always accompanied by a magnetic field. No one knows how the magnetic field is created or how it arises. But it always exists alongwith the electric field.

Why should not the same relationship be said to exist between body and consciousness ?"[40] Thus, the matter and consciousness are together. They are not separate from each other.

It is but the human being who determines, plans and constructs the social, economic and political structure of the society. Man has mental and physical power to do and undo anything. He cultivates, produces and distributes the agricultural and industrial products to the people. He has intellectual power to produce ethical, philosophical and cultural values to bring about all sided development of the people. He has tremendous imaginative, speculative and inquisitive power. Consequently, he has created society, religion, government, state, industries, culture and civilisation. Therefore, the poet-followers of Dr. Babasaheb Ambedkar described in the poetic dialect the Truth of the phenomenal world that the world is not based on the 'hood of the snake', as it is mythologically believed so by the Hindus, but it is based on the 'palms of the toilling masses'. Man has intuitive instinct of creation. Therefore, he created *epics* and *psalms*. Hence, the poetic genius describes that as 'Man was even before the Vedas. Thus, man is the creator of his own destiny and destination. Therefore, Dr. Babasaheb Ambedkar, following the Buddha states categorically that "the mind is the origin of all this is."[41] However, every man is not so strong to exibit his inner qualities due to adverse social circumstances, including adverse economic, educational and political circumstances. Indian society, especially is not open, nor liberal, nor progressive one. Therefore, the progress of the whole society in general and the backward communities in particular remained retarded to a great extent. "The aristocracy" said Babasaheb Ambedkar, "will have the resources derived from wealth and education. But this will not be the only advantage in favour of the aristocracy against which members of the minor and weaker communities have to struggle for their share of political power. There is another which though subtle in its operation is yet real. It consists in its social determinism. In this determinism there is no place for merit or ability. The only thing that counts is kinship which prompts the Indian to discriminate against persons who are not his kindred. The effects of this determinism operating in the minds of the members of the majority community is bound to put members of the smaller communities at a formidable disadvantage and may indeed forever shut them out from political power. The working out of this social determinism is bound to be most pernicious to the Depressed Classes."[42] Thus, a man's social status obviously determines his economic, educational, political and cultural status. In the Hindu social system, a Nandanar, or a Ravidas or a Chokha is an untouchable first and saint at the last.

(4) *Mechanism of Exploitation*:

Dr. Babasaheb Ambedkar had to split asunder the steel-frame mechanism of exploitation designed purposely by the *Brahmanic* forces in the remote past with the help of canonical text, fables, superstitious myths and legends so as to keep the majority of the meek people in the bondage of mental and physical slavery for protecting their own vested and selfish interests.

That mechanism was, however included the following elements.

(1) *Untouchability*:

Untouchability is a unique, inhuman and barbaric practice that proved to be most disadvantageous and injurious to the socalled untouchables in particular, and the Hindus in general. According to Dr. Babasaheb Ambedkar "untouchability was born sometime about 400 AD. It is born out of the struggle for supremacy between Buddhism and Brahmanism which has so completely moulded the

> history of India and the study of which is so woefully neglected by students of Indian history."[43]

The practice of untouchability was traced long back by some of the foreign Travellers in India; like Fa-hien (399 to 414 AD) Yuan-Chawang (629 to 645 AD), Al-Biruni (1017 to 1049), Duarte Barbosa (1500 to 1571); Jean de Thevenot (1666 to 1667), Fracois Bernier (1665 to 1668), Alexander Robertson (1938) Abbe J.A. Dubois (1792 to 1823) etc. Their writings reveal as to how untouchability was rampant in India and who were the victims of 'untouchability'. Even they had recorded what type of 'untouchability' was prevailing in those areas where they visited.[44]

What is 'untouchability' is a pertinent question. According to Dr. Babasaheb Ambedkar, "untouchability" is the notion of defilement, pollution, contamination and the ways and means of getting rid of that defilement. It is a case of permanent, hereditary stain which nothing can cleanse.[45]

In the words of Justice N. Sreenivas Rao, "the subject-matter of (Article 17) is not 'untouchability' in its literal or grammatical sense but the practice as it had developed historically in this country.

The use of the word 'untouchability' refers to the meaning of the term in the context of the historical development of the practice and does not connote its literal meaning.

A literal construction of the term would include persons who are treated as untouchables either temporarily or otherwise for various reasons, such as their suffering from an epidemic or contagious disease or on account of social observance such as are associated with birth or death or due to social boycott resulting from caste or other disputes.

'Untouchability' in such circumstances has no relation to the causes which relegated certain classes of people beyond the pale of the caste-system" (1958).[46]

In the words of Prof. Marc Galanter, In its broadest sense 'untouchability' might include all instances in which one person treated another as virtually unclean as a source of pollution.

A second and somewhat narrower sense of the term would include all instances in which a person was stigmatised as unclean or polluting or inferior because of his origin or membership in a particular group *i.e.* where he is subjected to invidious treatment because of difference in religion and membership in a lower or different caste.

Thus, we arrive at a third and still narrower sense of the term 'untouchability' as referring only to those practices concerned with the relegation of certain groups 'beyond the pale of the caste system' that is confining it to those disabilities imposed on groups commonly regarded as 'untouchables'.

'Untouchability' (then, as used in Article (17), is confined to invidious discrimination against certain not readily definable classes of persons." (1969)[47]

According to Dr. Babasaheb Ambedkar 'untouchability' and caste co-exist together, but both are virtually different from each other: (1) Caste system is based on Veda, Manusmriti and other religious scripture, whereas 'untouchability' is based on traditional contempt for Buddhism, and continuation of beef eating by the 'Broken men'; (2) When a Caste Hindu keeps social distance from other caste man, he observes caste system, but where he keeps social distance from the so-called low caste man, he observes 'untouchability'. (3) The caste of every Caste Hindu is a part of Caste system, but the Caste of an 'untouchable' is treated as beyond the pale of caste system. He is treated as out-caste.

According to Dr. Babasaheb Ambedkar 'slavery and untouchability' are two different institutions. 'Untouchability' came out of contempt and hatred against a particular community, whereas slavery has its origin in defeated men, sale or transfer, and born to a Dasi. Slavery is quite ancient whereas 'untouchability' is later invention. Slavery is universal but 'untouchability' is a special feature of Indian (Hindu) Society only. Untouchables were not only untouchables, but they were unapproachables and unseeables also. The slaves were allowed to perform domestic services in the houses of their masters. Their masters only were to control and dominate them; whereas the untouchables were traditionally at the service of the whole village. 'Untouchability' is a permanent stain, but the slavery was not so. The slaves were entitled to be free provided they fulfil certain conditions, for example, the war captives were allowed freedom if they replace other person, the debtors were allowed to be free if the debt is paid; they were set free if they saved the life of their master. Slavery is observed in respect of an individual, but 'untouchability' is observed in respect of the whole class or caste.

'Untouchability' can not be equated with poverty. Every untouchable may be poor, but every poor is not an untouchable. 'Untouchability' is a 'cause' whereas poverty is its 'effect'. Poverty is a common phenomenon with almost all the castes and communities, whereas 'untouchability' is related only to the lower or out caste, Hindu Caste. Poverty may not be necessarily permanent; with the change in circumstances poverty may be removed. Even a poor of the poor Caste Hindu is respected but not even a rich among the untouchables is respected. Even a person of the stature of Dr. Babasaheb Ambedkar could not get the services of peons or attendants in his office at Baroda in Gujarat. Even he was not allowed to fetch the water from the Chowdar Tank at Mahad in Raigad district in Maharashtra. The Caste Hindus alleged that his touch polluted the water of the tank and for purifying it they put in *'Panchgavya'*. The Caste Hindus did not allow him to enter the Kalaram Temple at Nasik, for which he had launched *Satyagraha* intermittantly for five years. What was it? Thus, it has amply proved that 'untouchability' was a permanent stain, which could not be cleansed by power, worth and postion. A poor caste man may not be economically able to purchase or avail some privilege, but he would be legally eligible to have that privilege; but not an untouchable.

Later on, 'untouchability' became notoriously conspicuous in the eighteenth century. It assumed a very virulent form of practice. It did not remain merely touch-me-notism, but assumed a form of unapproachability and unseeability. In the later part of eighteenth century during Raghunathrao Peshwa and Anandibai a farmar issues a or order was issued that the Mahar-an untouchable caste should walk on road with broom to remove their foot prints and they should bear a pot in the neck to spit in the same.[48] A proclamation was issued at Baroch in 1783 that no one of the three untouchable castes (halal khor, dhed and chandal) should come out of their houses after nine o'clock in the morning lest they would taint the air or touch the superior Hindus in the streets.[48(a)]

In Travancore, Kerala the untouchables were not allowed to wear clothes above the waist, "As far back as 1858 there were riots in Travancore because women converts to christianity took to wearing clothes above the waist."[49]

In 1857, a low caste *Khalasi*, by name Matadin Bhangi asked a *Brahman* Sepoy to let him drink water from his lota. The *Brahman* sepoy refused to give the Lota thinking that the touch of an untouchable *Khalasi* would defile it. Then the untouchable *Khalasi* angrily said, "you think much of your caste, but wait a little. The saheb log (Englishmen) will make you bite cartridges dipped in cow and pork fat, and then where will your caste be ?" Hence, the Braman Sepoy incidently came to know as to how they were boing polluted by the

British who asked to open the cartridges covered with it. That Brahman Sepoy Mangal Pandey ran through the barracks and instigated the Indian soldiers to rise in rebellion against the British regime as they were said to have been secretly defiling the Hindus as well as the Muslims. Thus, he ignited the flame of rebellion in 1857.[50]

These evil practices of 'untouchability' were not merely instances of exploitation, but of hatred and suppression of a community which later on known as the Scheduled Castes which comprised 429 castes and sub-castes in the erstwhile British India.[51] According to the first Census of 1881 out of 24,85,83,616 the untouchables were 4,30,92,200 forming 17.33 per cent of the total population of India. Now, 'untouchability' stands abolished under Article 17 of the Indian Constitution, 1950.

(2) *Devadasi System*

It seems that with the rise of Bhakti cult, there was corresponding rise in Devadasi System. In order to please and propitiate the fictitious divine power with the intention of achieving prosperity, credulous people started worshipping the God or Goddess in the form of idols with all divine attributes. Further in their bid to please the God more profusely, they invented the Devadasi system thinking the God would be more pleased by sensual pleasure offered by the Devadasis by their ritual dance, devotional songs, enchanting music and magnetic personality. The priests and feudals gave encouragement to the Devadasi system. They had naturally the vested interest in the system as they were to take actual pleasure of dancing girls and benefits of temple property. The priests were to get donations of land, gold, silver, diamonds *etc.*, and money for the maintenance of the temples, huge endowments, dancing girls, and the whole paraphernalia in the service of temple. The Devadasis were, however supposed to live in the temple premises and lead a spinster's life in the service of the deity and priests and feudal lords in the vicinity of the temple. They were presented to God as *Dasi* or Servant in a special ceremony performed by the priests alongwith other damsels and devotees. Since then the damsel was religiously assumed to be wife of the deity discharging all the services as wife. In the garb of a priest that wicked man was to abuse the chastity of the damsel or such damsel was assigned to any feudal Lord ready to make comparatively heavy payment for a night or for a stipulated period. Thus, the Devadasi was bound to live in the drudgery for her whole life without any hope to get the real life. Devadasi system was conspicuously prevalent in some parts of Kerala, Karnataka, Andhra, Maharashtra, West Bengal, Orissa and Assam. This system was mostly prevalent among the poor lower strata of the community. It was a source of income to the temple and a source of sensual pleasure to the wicked persons.

In order to realise the magnitude of the problem it would be worthwhile to give some references in this respect. The famous temple of Rajarajesvara at Thanjavur "had more than six hundred employees. Of them as many as four hundred were dancing girls."[52] During Cola Emperor Rajaraja (985-1016).

"Temple of Somanath which Mahamud of Gazani destroyed in 1026, had five hundred Devadasis, who provided music before the deity through out day and night."[53]

In Srikakulam in the Krishna district (A P), the temple of Vishnu had three hundred dancing girls attached to it in the twelfth century.[54]

These instances speak a lot about seriousness of the problem. This system continued further till 19th century with all its rigours and magnitude. Eventually, during the period of benevolent British Government, the Devadasi System was legally abolished under the

Indian Penal Code, 1860. The Government of Bombay passed the Bombay Devadasi, Protection, Act, 1934.

The Indian Penal Code, 1860 under its Section 372, and 373 provides punishment for immoral trafficking of any girl under the age of eighteen years. The Government of India passed "The Immoral Traffic (Prevention) Act, 1956."

Devadasi system, however still prevails in some parts of the country due to lack of specific legislation and proper implementation. It is a blot on humanity, as such it is better to remove it as soon as possible by making specific and an effective nation-wide law.

(3) *System of Involuntary Servitude*

In order to exploit the poor masses economically the *Brahmanic* forces brought in a system of involuntary servitude known in some parts of the country as *Baluta, Jajmani, Veti, Aya, Miliand,* and *Begari etc,.*

In the medieval period, village was the unit of administration. It was ruled by the head of the village known as Patil, Mukhia etc. He was representative of the king at the village level. He was, of course, invariably belonged to the land holding higher caste. His post was hereditary. He exercised great dominance over the whole village. He had to perform all the magisterial work at the village level. He used to order the services of any villager especially the Balutedar or Alutedar. They were necessarily belonged to the lower castes in the village. They were ordained to perform their respective caste occupation in the village society.

We get very authentic, systematic and detailed information regarding the village administration from the book in Marathi, entitled, *'Gaon-Gada'* written by Trimbak Narayan Atre in 1915. Accordingly "The Karu Naru who perform their duties based on their Caste and Skill for satisfying the general needs of the cultivators and of the whole village administration and the particular needs of the villagers for which they get a fixed share in the crops from the cultivators according to hereditory rules as remuneration is called respectively Baluta and Aluta."[55]

According to Owen M. Lynch, "*Jajmani System* is a co-operative system of production, distribution, and consumption. In its lower caste labourers and craftsmen worked for an upper caste patron and land owner. Membership in the system was hereditary and payment was in shares of grain, gifts of clothes, and soforth, which were distributed at set customany rates. In the traditional system, patron and clients were bound together not only by economic ties but also by ritual and political ones."[56]

In the words of Yogendra Singh, "inter-castes relations in villages are not only governed by relationship of dominance but also reciprocity. The institution which illustrates this phenomenon in the villages is the *Jajmani* System, also known as *Baluta, Aya, Miland,* etc,. in different regions of India. This institution has been the centre of economic and ritual mutuality and inter-dependence of castes binding them into relations ranging from dominance to reciprocity."[57]

Thus *Baluta* or *Jajmani* was a system of economic servitude and exploitation to the utmost extent. The worst sufferers of the system were the untouchable Mahars and such other castes. It was not based on 'contract' but hopelessly on 'status'. It was, however invented by the *Brahmanas* and the capitalist class to usurp the poor castes for no remunerative wages. It was more aggravative form of exploitation than usurping surplus value.

The *Balutedars* were included of twelve castes, *i.e., Mahar, Mang, Sonar* (goldsmith), *Sutar* (Carpenter), *Lohar* (Blacksmith), Chambhar (Cobbler), *Kumbhar* (Potmakers) *Nai* (Barber), *Dhobi* (Washerman), Gurav, *Halalkhor* (Scavenger) and *Joshi* (Fortune-teller).

Alutedars, who performed not very essential but auxiliary duties were eighteen in number. They were *Teli* (Oilman), *Tamboli* (Deal in betel leaf), *Sali* (Weavers), *Sangar*, Shimpi (*Tailor*), *Mali* (Gardener), *Gondhali, Dokrya, Bhat, Thakar, Gosavi, Jangam, Mulana, Vajantri, Ghadasi, Kalawant, Taral* and *Bhoi*.[58] Probably the castes would be different in different states. The *Baluta* or *Jajmani* system could give strength and support to village autonomy. Due to autonomous nature of village administration the villages were virtually isolated, independent, self-reliant and semi-sovereign. They did not care to know as to what is happening at the capital place, and to the national politics. Therefore, Dr. Babasaheb Ambedkar said very emphatically that, "These village republics have been the cause of the ruination of India.... what is the village, but a sink of localism, a den of ignorance, narrow-mindedness and communalism."[59]

(4) *Criminalisation of Certain Tribes*

It is a matter of great abomination to criminalise some of the Tribes. The Tribes are segregated communities. Like the untouchables they are also *Avarnas*. Due to the inhuman attitude of the Caste Hindus, they remained outside of the mainstream of the society having no permenant settlement, no source of livelihood, no education, culture and standard of living. Due to their victimisation, they turned to socially unacceptable means of livelihood. Therefore, they became subjects of contempt and ostracism to the mainstream society and the government.

In order to deal with the Criminal Tribes among the aborigines, the Criminal Tribes Act was passed in 1891. It however legally declared some of the tribes as criminals and put them under several inhuman restrictions. In 1911, under the new classification of criminal tribes, a new class of nomadic tribes was found. Later on under the constraints of the provisions of the

Constitution of India, the Criminal Tribes Act, 1871 was repealed in 1952, and in its place came the Habitual Offenders Act, 1952. Thus, the so-called criminal tribes were denotfied. However, they had to remain in the drudgery of in human restrictions for a longer period.

(5) *Hereditary Scavenging*

Scavenging is an unclean traditional occupation exclusively of a section of untouchables. It is a sort of aggravated form of untouchability imposed by the custom. It is the most ugly and injurious system, for which the scavengers were paid very meagre wages. They have no other means of livelihood. The whole generation is subjected to inhuman tradition followed by grinding poverty, illiteracy and segregation.

With a view to study the problem of the scavengers, the Government of India appointed two committees, both under the chairmanship of Mr. N.R. Malkani, who studied the problem and recommended to convert dry latrines into water-borne latrines for liberating the scavengers from that ugly occupation (1963). The commissioner for SC and ST had tried to pursue the government to remove this system.[60]

(6) *Law and Judiciary*

Society presupposes a certain legal system at its base. In the ancient and medieval period; the legal system was obviously based on *Sruti*, *Smriti*, *Dharmasutras* and *Commentaries* on law and judicial interpretations and social customs having validity. All the laws were written in Sanskrit; as such they were inaccesable to other *varnas* and castes, except the *Brahmanas*. The Brahmanas only had the privilege of learning Sanskrit. Therefore, the *Brahmanas* were to interprete the laws and the king was to deliver justice accordingly.

Of all the sources of Hindu Law, Manusmriti had assumed a primordial importance. *Sruti* was supposedly a divine source of law whereas Manusmriti was supposed to have based on religion. However, Smriti being based on Sruti, it also got the status of divine source; as such it was strictly observed in words and in spirit by almost all the Hindu Castes.

Manusmriti had specifically provided for rights, privileges and duties of the king and the men and women belonging to four *varnas* and liabilities of those outside of four varnas and castes. Every *varna* or caste had a different ritual status in caste system. In the words of Dr. Babasaheb Ambedkar, "The Indian society was formed with an ascending scale of reverence and a descending scale of contempt" and "gave no scope for the growth of the sentiment of equality and fraternity."[61]

> So far as Sudras are concerned Manu[62] laid down that,
>
> *Ekmeva Tu Shudrasya Prabhu : Karma Samadishat* |
>
> *Etasgameva Varnan Shushrushya Manasuyaya* | | (1:91)
>
> One occupation only the Lord prescribed to the Sudra, to serve meekly even these (other) three castes. (1:91)
>
> *Vistrabdham Brahmana Shudrad Dravyopadan macharet* |
>
> *Nahi Tashyasti Kinchitswam Bhartaharya dhano hi sa* | | (8:417)
>
> A Brahmana may confidently seize the goods of (his) Sudra (Slave); for, as that (Slave) can have no property, his master may take his possessions. (8:417)
>
> *Shaktenapi hi shudren na Karyo dhansanchaya* |

Shudro hi dhanama Sadhe
Brahmananeva badhate | | (10:129)

No collection of wealth must be made by a Sudra, even though he be able (to do it); for a Sudra who has acquired wealth; gives pain to Brahmanas. (X-129).

Thus, a Sudra had no civil-right to possess property. He was to serve all the upper castes and to receive that much which they pleased to give.

(7) *British Rule*

The British colonial rule in India was itself exploitative and oppressive. Dr. Babasaheb Ambedkar studied the system of financial management under the British rule in India and exposed its demerits.

In his book, 'Administration of Finance of the East-India Company' (1915), Dr. Babasaheb Ambedkar has precisely proved that the company's rule was disadvantageous to India. His critique of financial mismanagement by British was a great contribution to the Indian national movement and a great jolt to the colonial power. He said that from 1792-93 to 1857-58 the British East India Company had collected the revenue exorbitantly. He stated that from 1792-93 to 1855-56 the average annual land tax was 54.07, opium tax was 8.71, salt tax 11.07, Customs Revenue 6.22 and Miscellaneous tax was 15.90 per cent to the total revenue. This shows that agriculture was heavily taxed. So far as expenditure is concerned, during 1857, it had incurred 45.55 per cent on military, 7.19 per cent on interest of debt, 9.62 per cent on civil and political matter and 9.38 on judiciary.[63] Thus, the company had incurred heavy charges on military.

He had given the statistics relating to gross revenue and gross expenditure for all the sixty six years from 1792-93 to 1857-58, and proved that for most of the years there was surplus in revenue over expenditure. However, the government had not undertaken works beneficial to the public in general.

The company was paying divident to the share-holders of the company. They were living in luxury in England. Due to financial mismanagement company was bound to raise money by incurring loan and on bonds. They had not constructed canals or roads. They were raising tax on the essentials like salt. It had added nothing to the stock of gold and silver in India. By the Act of 1834, the company ceased to be a commercial corporation, but it continued in existence as a political sovereign of her Territories in India till the Mutiny of 1857. Ultimately, the rule of the company was taken over by the crown.

In his another thesis, *"The Evolution of Provincial Finance in British India"*published in 1925, Dr. Babasaheb Ambedkar gave an account of the evolution of the financial relations between the Imperial British Government and the provincial Governments from 1833 to 1923, and exposed in detail the exploitative nature of the of the financial policy of The British Government in India.

The Imperial System of Government in India dates from the year 1833, when the Act was passed to replace the existing 'multiplicity' in the system and to create an all powerful Central Government with the Governor-General in Council at Fort William in Bengal, legislating for and controlling the affairs of India as a whole. The Presidencies of Bombay and Madras were divested of their status and put them under the administration of the Governor and three Councillor for each of the Presidencies.

However, due to insufficient finance and heavy expenditure, the British Government decided to change 'United India into the United States of India ! and from a federal system for the Imperial System. The new system was thought to be advantageous as each province was to be responsible for administering its affairs within the funds alloted to it. The whole administrative system was revised according to the

Provisions of the Act of 1861. This gave rise to inauguration of provincial finance system in the year 1871-72.

From 1871-72 the necessary charges were granted by 'assignments' to the provinces. From 1877-78 to 1881-82 the provinces were alloted 'assigned revenues'; and 1882-83 to 1920-21, the Provincial Budget was based on 'shared revenues'.

He stated that from 1912-13 to 1916-17 the expenditure on District Administration was 6 per cent, on forest 1.9 per cent on opium etc. 6.2 per cent, debt 2.1 per cent, on civil deptarments 28.2 per cent, on civil charges 7.3 per cent and civil works 9.3 per cent, on Army 35.1 per cent and on finance and insurance it was 1.5 per cent (total 97.6 per cent).[64] Thus, the major portion of expenditure during the particular period was on the army and defence works.

So far as distribution of subjects was concerned, the Imperial Government controlled matters pertaining to military and defence affairs; foreign affairs, general taxation, currency, debt, tariffs, posts and telegraphs and audit and accounts; while the Provincial Government administered matters of ordinary internal administration, such as police, education, sanitation, irrigation, roads and buildings, forests and control over local bodies. However, the Provinces had very meagre sources of revenue with them. There was complete aggregation of the sources of revenue in the hands of the Government of India which distributed the yield of its taxes among the Provinces.

He obviously found that the bureaucrats were in charge of the whole administration. In his words, "The Indian Executive has sacrificed progress to order."[65] It was "taxing the masses and exempting the classes."[66] It increased the salt tax and land revenue and exploited the poor masses. It announced, "progressive realisation of responsible government" but failed to bring it into reality.

Conclusion

'Dialectical materialism' is a theory which leads to find out truth. Dialectic is a process which goes by opposites. It is thus a process of thesis, anti-thesis and synthesis. Hegel thought that the 'Idea' goes through the process of dialectism and ultimately culminates into the finding of absolute truth. Marx, however thought that it is not the 'idea', but the 'matter' which goes through the process of dialecticism. The world develops in accordance with the laws of movement of matter. He states that the material things are primary and mind and thoughts are secondary. It is not the consciouness of man, but his social existence decides his status in the society. Social and political revolutions originate not in mind, but with the change in mode of production. He thought that the matter or economic factors are behind the history. It is not any supernatural power, but the economic factors determine the economic status of the man.

It is because of extracting more labour, but rewarding less wages, the capitalists earn surplus value of the product. It is because of this exploitation the rich becomes richer and the poor becomes poorer.

According to Babasaheb Ambedkar discovery of truth is possible only when the mind is free to think, examine and reexamine the facts in the light of his scientific reasoning.

Following Buddha, Babasaheb Ambedkar said that matter and mind are not separate from each other. They are interdependent. He explained this phenomenon by citing the theory of 'Dependent Origination' enunciated by Buddha. He thought that it is not only economic factor responsible for historical development, but there are other factors like social, cultural, religious and environmental factors which are equally responsible for historical and political changes.

Babasaheb Ambedkar contemplates that it is because of the 'Steel Frame' mechanism of exploitation peculiar to Indian Society, some of the classes remained backward and downtrodden in India.

References and Notes

1. Volkov Genrikh: Birth of a Genius: pp. 222-223 Progress publishers, Moscow (1978).
2. Hunt Carew: 'The Theory and Practice of Communism': p. 27.
3. Doyle Phyllis: 'A History of Political Thought' p. 283. Jonathan Cape, Thirty Bedford Square, London (1933, 1963).
4. Volkov Generikh: 'Birth of a Genius': p. 234.
5. Kosambi D.D. Exhasperating Essays: p. 1. India Book Exchange, 38 Russa Rtd, Calcutta (Reprint 1977).
6. Marx Karl: Critique of Political Economy. p.11.
7. Marx Karl: Poverty of Philosophy p. 92. (Edited by : Martin Lawrence)
8. Sabine George H.A. *'History of Political Theory'* p. 766. Oxford & IBH Pub.Co. Calcutta. (3rd. 1961)
9. Marx Karl: *Capital* Vol. I. p. 1. George Allen and Unwin, London. (Edn.1949)
10. *Ibid.*, p. 2
11. *Ibid.*, p. 3
12. *Ibid.*, p. 7,8
13. *Ibid.*, p. 66
14. *Ibid.*, p. 106
15. *Ibid.*, p. 156
16. *Ibid.*, pp. 175-176
17. *Ibid.*, p. 194
18. *Ibid.*, p. 303
19. *Ibid.*, p. 304
20. An Article *'Buddhist Dialectics'* by Rahul Sankrutyayan in Buddhism: The Marxist Approach. p. 3. Peoples' Publishing House, Delhi. (1970)
21. *Ibid.*, Article "Bhuddhist Philosophy" by Y. Balaramamoorty. p. 44.
22. *Ibid.*, p. 27
23. Goyenka Satyanarayan: Kya Buddha Nastik the? p. 86. *Atta hi Attano Natho, Ko hi Natho Paro Siya ! Vipashyana Vishodhan Vinyas. Dhammagiri Igatpuri,* Maharashtra. (2008)
24. Article by Y. Balaramamoorty in *"Buddhism the Marxist Approach".* p. 38
25. *Ibid.* p. 39

26. Murty K. Sachidanand: Nagarjuna. p. 80
National Book Trust, India, New Delhi. (Reprint 1983)
27. An Article by Y. Balaramamoorty in Buddhism the Marxist Approach, p. 50
28. Murty K. Sachidanand: Nagarjuna, pp. 80-81
29. DBAWS Vol. II, pp. 240-241
30. *Ibid.* p. 89
31. Narasu P. Lakshmi: The Essence of Buddhism, pp. 58-59
Buddha Bhumi Prakashan, Kamptee Rtd; Nagpur (2nd Edn. 2002)
32. DBAWS, Vol. I, p. 212.
33. *Ibid.,* p. 213.
34. *Ibid.,* p. 43
35. *Ibid.,* p. 44
36. *Ibid.,* Vol. VII, p. 379
37. *Ibid.,* p. 274
38. Keer Dhananjay-Malashe: Mahatma Phule: Samagra Vangmay, p. 189.
Maharashtra Rajya Sahitya Ani Sanskriti Mandal, Mumbai (1980).
39. DBAWS, Vol. II. p. 255.
40. *Ibid.,* pp. 262-263
41. *Ibid.,* p. 282
42. Khairmode C.B. Dr. Bhimrao Ramji Ambedkar Biography, Vol. IV, p. 23.
Dr. Ambedkar Education Society, Tulsipipe Road, Mumbai, 13 (1966).
43. *DBAWS*. Vol. II, p. 379.
44. For details see, 'Rise of Self-consciousness Among the untouchables in Ancient and Medieval India' by Dr. R.K. Kshirsagar, pp. 44-41.
Kaushalya Publication, HUDCo, Aurangabad (2008).
45. DBAWS, Vol.VII: pp. 249, 266.
46. AIR 1958 Mysore (*Devarajiah* Vs. *Padmanna*)
47. An article "The abolition of disabilities - untouchability and the Law." Marc Galantc in the untouchables in contemparary India. p. 243, 244, 245,246. Edited by Miachel Mahar.
The University of Arizona Press, Arizona, USA (1969).
48. For details sec, *"Untouchability in India*—Implementation of the Law and Abolition; by Dr. R. K. Kshirsagar, pp. 39-40.
Deep and Deep Publications, Rajouri Garden, New Delhi. (1986).

48(a) 'O' Malley L.S.S: 'Indian Caste Customes. p. 147. Vikas Publishing House, Delhi (1932, 1974)
49. 'O' Malley L.S.S. 'Indian Caste Customes', p. 154.
50. For details see dalit Movement in India and its Leaders," by Dr. R. K. Kshirsagar, p. 112.
M.D. Publications Pvt. Ltd. 11 Darya Ganj, New Delhi. (1994)
51. DBAWS, Vol. VII. pp. 259-265.
52. Prasad A. K. Devadasi System in Ancient India. p. 55.
HK Publishers, A-1/11 Shakti Nagar Extension, Delhi (1990).
53. *Ibid.,* p. 41.
54. *Ibid.,* p. 67.
55. Atre Trimbak Narayan. Gaon-Gada P.13
Varad Books 'Varada' Senapati Bapat Marg, Pune (1915, 1989).
56. Lynch Owen *M: The Politics of Untouchability* p. 35 (notes) National Publishing House, Darya Ganj, Delhi (Edn. 1974)
57. Singh Yogendra: *Modernization of Indian Tradition*. p. 186. Rawat Publications, Jawahar Nagar Vaijpur (1986)
58. Atre Trimbak Narayan: Gaon-Gada. pp. 14-15.
59. DBAWS Vol.- 3, p. 62.
60. For details see Annual Report (2009-2010), published by the Ministry of Social Justice and Empowerment Goverment of India (Part-I, p. 47).
61. DBAWS: Vol. I, p. 51.
62. Buhler G. Laws of Manu. (1886, 1964)
Motilal Banarsidas, Jawahar Nagar, Delhi-6.
63. DBAWS: Vol. VI, p. 25.
64. *Ibid.,* p. 232.
65. *Ibid.,* p. 228.
66. *Ibid.,* p. 229.

4

Thoughts on Society

According to Aristotle, 'man is by nature and necessity a social animal'. Thus, society is quite natural, essential, eternal and universal. It is instrumental in evolving an atmosphere which would be conducive not only for the satisfaction of his primary wants, but for the development of his personality. However, the structure of society is not common everywhere. Society is a repository of social values, culture and civilisation and it transmits the same to the next generation. It is responsible not only for continuity of mankind but continuity of culture and civilisation.

Presently, no society is fully based on kinship. It has lost its homogenity quite long back. Previously, the society was based on kinship, religion, common territory and language and common social habits. Thus, the society was divided on many counts. However, with development of science, means of production, means of communication, development of trade and education and better avenues of life the composite nature of society gave place to the diversified nature of society. According to Dr. Babasaheb Ambedkar, "Men do not become a society by living in physical proximity any more than a man ceases to be a member of his society by living so many miles away from other men. Secondly, mere similarity in certain habits and custom is not enough to constitute a society. Parallel activity, even if similar, is not sufficient to bind men into society."[1] For constituting society what is necessary is "to share and participate in a common activity so that the same emotions are aroused in him that animate the others. Making the individual a sharer or partner in the associated activity so that he feels its success as his success, its failure as his failure is the real thing that binds men and makes a society of them."[2] Thus, society is based on "cordial inter-relationship" among the human beings constituting it, irrespective of common territory, common language common tradition and history and common religion.

A (1) Class-society

There is however much more difference, between the class society and the caste society.

1. In the class society there are obviously three classes: Rich or higher class, Middle class, and poor or artisan class. Membership of class is based on economic condition of the people.
2. In class-society there is no rigid hierarchy. They do not observe a definite system of social precedence over the other classes. There are gradations in the society but they are obviously based on relations in property.
3. In the words of Thomas Mathew, "the most crucial aspect of the Marxian category of 'class' is consciousness. It is not just an economic or social category. Without ideological content, 'class' is meaningless even as an analytical category. There is hardly any need to emphasise the importance of consciousness in class formation, class struggle and social revolution. The point I am trying to make is that 'class' is not just an economic, social or racial category as generally understood. It is a dynamic concept with an ever-vibrant soul, consciousness."[2(a)]
4. The class-based social structure is not permanent as such, it may change possibly with the change in economic condition of the people. The social relations correspondingly change with the change in property relations. They do not believe that socio-economic condition is the creation of super natural power or God. In India social structure is permanent. It can not be changed or altered. It is believed that it is based on vedas. Thus, it is supposed to be the creation of the God

Brahma. Moreover, it is said that the birth in a particular caste is based on the *Karma Sanchit* or *The Karma* in the past life.

5. In the class-society there are no restrictions as such in the matter of social intercourse. There are not restrictions on inter-dining and inter-marriages. Inter-course among them is a matter of their personal choice without social restrictions.

   Whereas in Indian Caste Society social-inter course like inter-dining and inter-marriages are subject to religious rules and restrictions. They can not go against the rule of endogamy, otherwise they have to face social boycott. Every caste has its elderly body known as 'Panchayat' which deals with caste disputes and family disputes.

6. In the class-society, people are free to reside in any part of the town. There can not be separate locality for any class as such.

   In the caste-society separate localities are marked for each caste. The so-called untouchable castes live in segregated localities somewhat detached from the main village or town. They are culturally also segragated from the touchable castes. They can not take part in social and religious programmes of the touchable castes.

7. In the class-society every person is at liberty to perform or adopt the avocation of his choice, subject to his ability and availability of opportunities. "Society is, according to D.D. Kosambi," "held together by the bonds of production."[3]

   Whereas in the caste society every person is bound to perform his caste occupation as determined by the *Shastras*. Moreover, it is given to understand that there lies salvation only in performing one's own occupation.

[2] Class-struggle

Karl Marx has most emphatically observed in his *Communist Manifesto* (1948) that, "the history of all hitherto existing society is the history of class struggles."[3(a)] There has been constant conflict of interests between the Haves and Have notes. In the modern age those classes are known as Bourgeoisie and Proletariat.

In the words of Karl Marx, "By Bourgeoisie is meant the class of modern capitalists, owners of the means of social production and employers of wage labour."[4] The class of Bourgeoisie has sprouted from the ruins of feudal society; but it has not done away with the traditional antagonism prevailing in the society. Even it has established new classes and new conditions of oppressions, thereby gave rise to new forms of struggle in place of the old ones. Modern industrialism, market conditions, monopolising over means of productions and insatiable want of profiteering, increasing consumerism gave rise to exploitation and oppression of the working men in industries and agricultural fields. This caused the split of the society into two self-opposing camps known as Bourgeoisie and Proletariat, Haves and Have-nots. "By proletariat, is meant, the class of modern wage labourers who, having no means of production of their own, are reduced to selling their labour power in order to live."[5] According to Karl Marx, there has been and is fierce struggle between these two classes for protection of their own class-interests. The Bourgeoisie are in minority and the proletariats are in majority, but the Bourgeoisie proved to be powerful because they own and control the means of production and the state is always in their support. Even, the Bourgeoisie "has converted the physician, the lawyer, the priest, the poet, the man of science into its paid wage-labourers."[6] Even, it has "reduced the family relation to a mere money relation."[7]

In order to earn more and more profit and amassed capital, the Bourgeoisie constantly revolutionise the instrument of production expand market for its products, develop the means of communication and brings out large scale production and earns more and more surplus value. On the contrary, the lower strata of the middle class including the petty shopkeepers, peasants and workers "Sink gradually into the Proletariat." Both, the Bourgioisie and the Proletariat struggle for protecting their vested and conflicting interest. This, of course gives rise to class struggle.

Marx enunciates the theory of economic determinism. He states that the mode of production at any given time explains its political and indeed its whole cultural condition at that time in a particular state. The capitalist mode of production, ultimately divide the society into capitalist and proletariat classes. In the capitalistic society, the capitalists try to obtain more and more profit by increasing surplus value.

In order to understand the meaning of 'surplus value' it is imperative to understate the meaning of labour theory of value given by Karl Marx. He begins with analysing the commodity as an article which has utility which is the product of human labour and is produced for the market. The commodity is expressed in terms of exchange value in the market; which is governed by the quality of 'socially necessary' labour. The socially necessary labour involves four propositions.

(1) The socially necessary labour time means the time spent by labour possessing average skill, efficiency and intensity.

(2) It includes the normal conditions of production, supported by modern machinery.

(3) The product being produced must be in demand.

(4) The labour time counted must include past labour used on raw material and machinery and present labour for producing the product. Thus, Marx considered labour as a source of value being the sole productive factor.

Marx pointed out that, the capitalist in order to operate the material means of production with him, will purchase the labour power of the labourer. However, the wages which pays are not equivalent to the exchange value of the product. The value of the labour is determined on the basis of number of hours put in for producing the particular commodity and not on the basis of exchange value of the commodity. Thus, the surplus value means, "The difference between what the worker receives in wages and the value of the commodity he produces."[8] This difference they keep on increasing, thereby obtaining increased absolute surplus value. The problem is the worker does not own the means of production; or possesses very marginalised means of production. Ultimately, he goes to market with a commodity for sale his capacity to work, his labour power. That is what the employer buys from him. That is what the employer pays him wages for the worker sell his commodity, labour power, to the boss in return for wages. The workers will get in return for their labour power, subsistence wages and not sufficient wages.

"These productive forces are concentrated in the hands of a few bourgeoisie whilst the great mass of the people are more and more becoming proletarians, and their condition more wretched and unendurable in the same measure in which the riches of the bourgeoisie increase.[9] Consequently, the richer becomes more rich and poor becomes more poor and the gap continues to increase.

The doctrine of class structure, "according to R. P. Sharma, is, a myth. There has never been natural proletarian solidarity in history."[10] He further states that, "A free society must be ready to tolerate differences; differences are rather the very breath of freedom. The so-called unity of interests of the proletariat is a mere fiction."[11]

In Europe, the economy was industrialised. Therefore, there could have existed Bourgeoisie and Proletariat classes. Indian economy being agrarian there were landlords, peasants and agricultural tenants. All of them were under the supremacy of the Brahmin class or priestly class; irrespective of their economic status.

Under the British colonial rule the new land system was ushered in with *Zamindari, Rayatwari* and *Mahalwari*. By creating individual holders of land, it intrduced the system of individual land assessment and revenue payment. Thus, after the advent of colonial rule the old agrarian system was abolished, thereby the village autonomy was also abolished. However, this gave rise to parasitic land owning class and actual tenant class; but is fully divided into castes and sub-castes. So there could not arise class-consciousness.

Karl Marx seems to be aware of more than two classes, like "freemen and slave, patrician" and plebeian, Lord and Serf, guild master and journeyman: However, he puts all those existing classes into two main intrinsically opposite classes, they are — "oppressor and oppressed," who "stood in constant opposition to one another, carried on an uninterrupted, now hidden now open fight, a fight that each time ended either in a revolutionary reconstitution of society at large, or in the common ruin of the contending classes." Thus, he was aware of the complexity of social structure.

The class-struggle existed previously, according to him, is still in existence. In the modern age, there are Proletariat and Bourgerisie classes. They are constantly opposing each other in their bid to protect their own interests. Karl Marx views world history, not as a record of wars between nations, kings or generals, but as a succession of struggles between opposing classes for economic hegemony.

[3] Diagnosis of the Problem of Class-society

Karl Marx has obviously viewed the problem of the Proletariat from the materialistic point of view. He observed from the very close corner that the Proletariat class was desperately suffering from acute poverty due to exploitation and oppression from the capitalist class, priestly class and the state machinery. He has stated certain instances of exploitation of the labourers in his famous book *Communist Manifesto*, which are very heart- rending. Marx thought very rationally on the state of affairs of the Proletariat and rightly found that the bourgioisie class was responsible for all the agonies as they had unsatisble lust to grab more and more profit and exploit the moral and material things from the Proletariat. He thought the economic forces which were fully under the control of the bourgioisie class were the main cause of their sufferings.

He thought that Proletariat revolution was only befitting remedy over the situation. He said, "the Communists disdain to conceal their views and aims. They openly declare that their ends can be attained only by the forcible overthrow of all existing social conditions. Let the ruling classes tremble at a Communist revolution. The Proletarians have nothing to lose but their chains. They have a world to win. Working men of all countries unite!"[12] Subsequently, he wants to acquire political power and establish socialislistic state, wherein all the instruments of production would be owned by the state, everybody would be able to get that is needed to him and work as per his capacity and worth.

Karl Marx gave importance to acquisition of political power by the Proletariat. He said very categorically that, "The seizure of political power by the working class is the first step in the revolution. The second step is to recast the social order and to crush the resistance of the capitalist class to the change."[13]

Thus, Marx attributes all the miseries of the Proletariat to economic factors, but finds solution in political power. He contemplates that political power is *sine-quo-non* of all the remedies. He thinks that with strength of political power the working class would be able to remove all the fetters and obstacles in the way of establishment of a new social order.

Lenin also subscribes vehemently to the proposition of Marx that political power is essential to establish a new political order wedded to socialism. He states that, "the first step in the revolution by the working class is to raise the Proletariat to the position of ruling class, to win the battle of democracy."[14]

B. [2] Caste Society

1. It is imperative to acquaint with the Caste System in India as it is a root cause of poverty and social-inequality. The characteristic features of Hindu Society, according to G. S. Ghurye, are as under:

   (i) *Segmental division of society:* The caste society is not a homogeneous community. Every caste has its own life, the membership is based on birth. The status of a person depend not on his wealth as in the classes of modern Europe, but on the traditional importance of the caste in which a person is born. Every caste follows its ascribed vocation. Every caste has its elderly body known as panchayat which deals with caste disputes including family disputes.

(ii) *Hierarchy*: The castes observe a definite system of social precedence amongst the castes; with *Brahmin* at the top, followed by *Kshatriya*, *Vaishya* and *Shudras* and other intermediate castes. The so called untouchables form the fifth place but outside the *varna* system.

(iii) *Restrictions on feeding and social inter-course*: There are certain rules and restrictions on feeding. The food given by Dwija Caste only is treated pure and accepted by all. The food from lower casts is not acceptable to the higher castes. There are no social relations among the castes.

(iv) *Civil and religious disabilities*: The people in the villages reside in separate localities. The so called untouchable castes live in segregated localities. They can not take part in social and religious programmes. They have to keep distance from the congregation of the Caste Hindus.

(v) *Lack of unrestricted choice of occupation*: The castes are bound to perform their hereditary occupations and it is believed that, there lies their salvation only in their caste occupation. Therefore there could not be occupational mobility in the caste society.

(vi) *Restrictions on marriage*: Marriages with a person of that particular castes are allowed. In other words there is perfect endogamy among the equals only. Any transgression of this rule is regarded as a breach of caste and religious rule subject to social boycott.[14(a)]

Thus, the caste system which has been prevailing in India is a unique, unparalleled and most oppressive one. It is considered as based on Vedas, Smritis and Custom. Hindu Caste society is a steel-frame organisation. Although it has accepted some of the very minor changes over a period of time; its outer-structure and inner-hatred for the so-called inferior castes remained in tact.

In the Indian socio-economic situation surplus value has virtually no significance. There was production, but not commodity or exchange value. Every caste, especially the lower castes were expected to offer their services as and when called for by the so-called high caste people without any remuneration or with very little remuneration, and it was given in the form of some corn or crumbs. They were not to question why, but to do and die without remorse to anyone. The lower castes were not expected to earn wealth. The *Brahmin* caste was authorised to snatch away any property or thing from the lower castes. They had no right to own any property.

[2] Caste-struggle

The statement of Karl Marx, *i.e,*. "the history of all hitherto existing society is the history of class-struggle," might be true in respect of other countries, but it can not be so in respect of India. According to Dr. Babasaheb Ambekar, Indian Society is obviously a caste society. Caste in its beginning might be a class, but when it was closed from outside, it became caste, closed for both insiders to go out and outsiders to come in for ever. The Hindu Society, a major component of Indian society is but, "a collection of castes. Each caste is conscious of its existence."[15] "The caste system, he states, prevents common activity and by preventing common activity it has prevented the Hindus from becoming a society with a unified life and a consciousness of its own being."[16]

He states that the caste system is not a 'division of labour'[17] which is a necessary feature of every civilised society, but it is a division of labourers which is unnatural and uneconomic. It compels its members to accept only 'predestined occupations,' and restricts their freedom of occupation.

Dr. Babasaheb Ambedkar being an atheist and a rationalist to the core did not believe in the divine origin of caste system and untouchability. According to him the *Brahman* or the priestly class in order to maintain its superiority over the existing classes observed the rule of endogamy very strictly. The remaining classes in society were constrained to imitate the Brahmin Caste and developed the rigid custom of endogamy which resulted in emergence of castes. The Manusmriti gave religious sanction in a bid to justify it, and provided strict rules and regulations to be followed by various castes in order to consolidate caste-system.

The caste is an "enclosed class". Its membership is based on birth. Members of the caste observe the rule of endogamy. They prohibit inter-dining. They have to undertake the avocation of their caste. Generally, they reside in a particular locality in the village or town. They are governed by the rules, regulation and custom of their caste. They observe the manners, etiquetts of their caste and accept the supremacy of Shastras and *Brahmanas*. Whereas a class-society is a open society where no restrictions customary to the caste-society are observed. However, they observe certain common manners and etiquetts for the good of all.

In the class-society there could be class-struggle caused by economic forces; but in the caste-society there could be caste-struggle based on caste prejudices and caste status. Indian society being a caste society there have been caste-struggles. However, due to imposed illiteracy, poverty and restrictions to bear arms, they could not wage a war against the priestly class and feudal class and defeat them finally. The close study of Indian history, however reveals that the unfair play of *Brahmanic* forces were at the root of every historical event. Almost every caste is not only envious to other caste, but it is virtually an arch enemy of other caste. However, due to socio-religious reforms certain changes are being taking place in the caste attitude, structure and values.

In this background, the statement made by Karl-Marx, that, "The history of all hitherto existing society is the history of class-struggle", seems to be half-truth. Dr. Babasaheb Ambedkar did not subscribe to this observation by Karl Marx.

[3] Diagnosis of the Problem of Caste Society and the Untouchability

As Indian society could be characterised as a Caste-Society, so also the Indian economy could be characterised as a Caste-economy. In India, the caste decides the profession and economic status of a man. One has to strictly adhere to the caste rules. One can not change his profession, nor it is religous to change it. By performing one's own avocation he may get salvation. It may be 'True in European Society' that exploitation was the natural consequence of the laissez-faire policy, industrialisation and usurpation of surplus value. So far as Indian Society is concerned it is not so. In India exploitation is the result of Hindu religious system and it has been in existence since time immemorial.

Babasaheb Ambedkar was undoubtedly fully aware of the fact that the Dalits suffer from poverty and inadequacy. He thought that the system like *Mahar Watan* was grinding the poor Depressed Classes. Hence, he tried to get it abolished. He wanted to distribute the barren land to the Dalits for cultivation. He wanted nationalisation of agricultural land and establish corporations like insurance. He formed the Independent Labour Party for the uplift of labour class including mostly the Depressed Classes. Thus, he stood for economic uplift of Depressed Classes as such as any other socialist leader. However, he gave more importance to their emancipation from slavery, illiteracy, gender inequality and priesthood. He said very categorically that, "self-respect is more important than the material gains, our struggle is for honour, for self-respect, not only for the economic progress."[18]

Dr. Babasaheb Ambedkar has rightly observed that, "we can..... say with some confidence that untouchability was born some time about 400 AD. It born out of the struggle for supremacy between Buddhism and Brahmanism which has so completely moulded the history of India...." Thus, it was the struggle between Buddhists and the Brahmanas for supremacy which resulted in the origin of 'untouchability'. It was the hatred of the *'Brahmamas'* against the Buddhists which gave rise to *untouchability*. The other communities, however accepted the supremacy of the *Brahmanas*, but the so called 'Broken Men' who were Buddhists were not agreeable to accept it. Therefore, the *Brahmanas* imposed *'untouchability'* to subdue them.

Therefore, Babasaheb Ambedkar thought that the problem of the Depressed Classes was, obviously political rather than economic, whereas the problem of Proletariat in the opinion of Karl Marx, was economic. The caste system generates the sense of superiority or inferiority in relation to others not because one caste is economically rich other is poor; but because one feels superior or inferior as a principle of caste system provided in the *shastras*. In respect of caste status economic condition is irrelevant. Therefore, while describing the nature of the problem of the Depressed Classes Dr. Babasaheb Ambedkar had said that, "we are often reminded that the problem of the Depressed Classes is a social problem and that its solution lies elsewhere than in politics. We take strong exception to this view. We hold the problem of the Depressed Classes will never be solved unless they get political power in their own hands."[19] Therefore, he put forth the demand of separate electorate for the Depressed Classes, so as to get adequate and effective representation in the Legislature.

The ills of both the society being unidentical, one can not expect that the diagnosis of those ills should be identical. No Proletarian might have met the fate of an untouchable. The sense of caste purity is so deeply rooted in the Indian people, that even the place in Agakhan Palace was got purified, which was allegedly polluted by the visit of Babasaheb Ambedkar during the negotiations leading to

Poona Pact.[20] When Shri Jagjivan Ram, the then Minister in the Central Government unveiled the statue of Sampurnanand at Varanasi, the Caste Hindus felt that it was polluted by the touch of an untouchable, as such they purified it by pouring ganga-water thereon.[21] These were specifically the problem of *'untouchability'* which were naturally unknown to the class-society.

It seems that, Marx probably was not well-aware of the Hindu Social Structure and the norms. He dislikes the British bourgeoisie for their colonial rule in India; but ennobles the *Brahmin,* who had wantonly created the castebased social structure for exploitation and oppression of the socalled lower classes.[22]

The caste system including *varna* system is the very foundation of Hinduism. Therefore, for a Hindu protagonist it is difficult to go against the caste system. However, progressive and rationalist he might be, he can not destory the caste at the cost of his religion.

The incident in the life of Marx when the landlady driven out Jenny and her child due to inability of paying the rent of the house reminds us of the similar incident in the life of Babasaheb Ambedkar, when he was driven out of a room on the ground of being a man of 'despicable' caste in 1917 at Baroda. The first incident was based on economic inability to pay the rent whereas later was based on 'untouchability.' This is the difference between 'class' and 'caste'!

In the words of R.R. Bhole (J) "Dr. Ambedkar did not agree with the theory enunciated by Karl Marx and differed from him in that the sufferings in this country are not only due to economic exploitation but also due to social exploitation and degradation."[23]

In the words of Dr. N.D. Kamble, "The poverty and inequality in India are the two sides of the same coin; originating from *varna* system or caste system and its *Varnashram Dharma.* Inequalities and poverty need not necessarily co-exist, but the experience in India shows that both of them co-eisted since centuries and are co-existing even today."[24]

Dr. Babasaheb Ambedkar had a definite vision of an ideal society. His ideal society is based on liberty, equality and fraternity; where there would be perfect endosmosis. He said, "An ideal society should be mobile, should be full of channels for conveying a change taking place in one part to other parts. In an ideal society there should by many interests consciously communicated and shared. There should be varied and free points of contact with other modes of association."[25]

Conclusion

There are, of course certain differences between the two social systems. In Europe it is the poverty and in India it is the Caste System which had divided the society in two conflicting groups.

However, both the thinkers, Karl Marx and Babasaheb Ambedkar State in almost unanimous tone that there has been constant struggle between the exploiting class and the exploited class in the respective society.

The struggle between the two classes or castes was caused by the exploitative system developed with the connivance of capitalists, priestly class and feudals in both the situations for safeguarding their own selfish interests.

Both the thinkers thought that the victims of the exploitative system must unite together in a formidable force and revolt against the whole exploitative system and capture power for their liberation.

Notes and References

1. DBAWS: Vol.I : p. 51.
2. *Ibid.,:* p. 51.
2a. Mathew Thomas: Re-reading Ambedkar. p. 49. Samyak Prakashan Paschimpuri, New Delhi (2007).
3. Kosambi D.D., and *Exasperating Essays* : p. 2.
3a. Marx Karl and Engels: *Manifesto of the Communist Party,* p. 41, (2012).
4. *Ibid,.*: notes (1)
5. *Ibid,.*: p. 40.
6. *Ibid,.*: p. 45.

7. *Ibid,.*: p. 45.
8. Huberman Leo: *Introduction to Socialism*, p. 24.
9. Marx-Engels: *The Socialist Revolution*, p. 49.
   Progress Publishers, New Delhi, p. 1978.
10. Sharma R.P. Modern Western Political Thought, p. 361.
11. *Ibid.*, p. 362.
12. Marx-Engels: Manifesto, p. 96 (2012).
13. Huberman Leo-Sweezy Paul: *Introduction to Socialism*, p. 77.
14. Lenin: *The State and Revolution*, p. 25.
14a. Ghurye G.S.: Caste and Race in India. pp. 2-28.
   Popular Prakashan (Rep. 1988) Bombay.
15. DBAWS: Vol.I: p. 50.
16. DBAWS: Vol.I: p. 51.
17. DBAWS: Vol.I: p. 47.
18. Das Bhagwan: (Ed.) *Thus Spoke Ambedkar*, Vol. II, p. 145.
19. DBAWS. Vol. 2, p. 506.
20. Sanjana J.E. Caste and Out-Caste, p. 32 (1946).
21. Dinman - 12-18 Feb. 1978.
22. For details see, the Socialist Revolution by Marx-Engels. pp. 106-107 (1978).
23. Forward by Justice Bhole to Bhimrao Ramji Ambedkar: A Study in Social Democracy, by Dr. G.S. Lokhande. Intellectual Publishing House, Darya Ganj, New Delhi (1977).
24. Kamble N.D. *Roots of Poverty in India.* p.11 Aurangabad, (1982).
25. DBAWS .Vol. I: p. 57.

5

Thoughts on Religion

What is religion is a pertinent question which needs to be addressed. From etymological point of view 'Religion' is derived from the Latin word, *'Religare'* which means to bind together.[1] Thus, which binds together the mass of people under an association is religion. According to Emile Durkheim, religion is, "a unified system of beliefs and practices relative to sacred things, uniting into a single moral community all those who adhere to those beliefs and practices."[2]

People generally believe that there is God and it decides the fate of human beings. In order to attract the blessings of God, people go to any extent to propitiate God. They think it is God who dictates and nobody has any power to change it. They get either heaven or hell at the will or curse of God. In their bid to please God, they spend their energy, property and any pleasure. Of course, what is religion is what the priest decides. With this understanding the priesthood and vested interests came into existence. Priest is known as representative of God on earth. The capitalists please the priestly class by giving huge donations etc. Therefore, they are always with the capitalists. They propagate that it is because of curse of God, some people are poor. Poverty could be eradicated by serving the interests of the priestly class and not by raising any protest against the exploitation. Thus, the propertied class and the priestly class have formed the alliance for protecting their vested interests. However, the rationalist thinker's do not believe in religion, God, hell or heaven or past *Karma* or cures.

[A] Karl Marx on Religion

Karl Marx did not believe in religion, God and superstitions having no rational explanation. "Marx resolutely proclaimed human self-consciousness as the "highest divinity."[3] He thought that "The roots of religion are" earthly "in origin. Religious mediocrity is an expression of the real mediocrity of social relations."[4]

Man has intellectual and physical capacity to develop his personality and change sorrounding condition suitable to his survival. However, the "God-s-slaves" do not trust themselves. "Feeling weak and helpless in the struggle for his liberation and the struggle with nature, man invests God with power and omnipotence. Man seeks in God compensation for the wretchedness of his own existence."[5] Marx thought that "Lack of reason is the existence of god."[6] In the words of Yuri Sdobnikov "the emergence of belief in the gods was a reflection of the first stage in the development of human consciousness, a primitive level of thinking which was still incapable of understanding and explaining the sorrounding world and which ascribed to it supernatural and irrational properties. "Marx pointed out that, "for whom the world appears without reason, hence who is without reason himself, for him God exists."[7]

However, the propertied class and the priestly class are in an unjust alliance at the cost of toiling masses. Therefore, Karl Marx thought that religion is a opium of the people. It has always been an ally of the forces of power, the propertied classes. "Marx proclaimed atheism to be his creed."[8]

Marx observed certain practices of the Christians and jews in Europe and thought that they are anti-social.[8(a)] He thought that religion is the product of primitive society caused by ignorance. Therefore they had no rational explanation for the formidable forces of nature. According to Marx, "Man makes religion, religion does not make man."[9] In the words of A Barmenkov, "The ruling classes adopted religious ideology as a tool to maintain and strengthen social inequality."[10]

However, with the rise of rationalism science and atheism, religion is subjected to scathy criticism. Marx and Engels thought that religion is an obstacle in the way of socialism and scientific inquiry.

According to Karl Marx, "The basis of irreligious criticism is: "Man makes religion, religion does not make man. Religion is the self-consciousness and self-esteem of man, who has either not yet found himself or has already lost himself again. But man is not abstract being encamped outside the world. Man is the world of man, the state, society. This state, this society, produce religion, an inverted world-consciousness, because, they are an inverted world. Religion is the general theory of that world, its encyclopaedic compendium, its logic in a popular form, its spiritual *point d'honneur,'* its enthusiasm, its moral sanction, its solemn complement, its universal source of consolation and justification. It is the fantastic realisation of the human essence because the human essence has no true reality. The struggle against religion is therefore indirectly a fight against the world of which religion is the spiritual aroma.

Religious distress is at the same time the expression of real distress and also the protest against real distress. According to Marx "Religion is the sigh of the oppressed creature; the heartless of a heartless world, just as it is the spirit of spiritless conditions. It is the opium of the people."[11]

In the words of A. Barmenkov, "Ideologists of the church deny that religion's main function is to justify and defend social inequality. They try to persuade the toiling masses that suffering is mankind's eternal fate, that social inequality and injustice have been established by God and are the result of man's fall."[12]

He further states that, "The acceptance and defence of the exploitation of man by man reflect the social essence of religion. In as much as social inequality has been established by God, it says, it would be senseless to resist social injustice. To seek to alter the social order is to apostatise. To please the ruling classes, ministers of all religions teach believers that the majority of the people cannot expect terrestrial happiness; but can only hope for paradise beyond the grave. The church has always done everything in its power to divert the working people from class-struggle."[13]

[B] Babasaheb Ambedkar on Religion

Dr. Babasaheb Ambedkar's approach towards religion is rational, social and utilitarian. He did not believe in traditional and popular concept of religion; which is, in his own words, "belief in God, belief in Soul, worship of God, curing of the erring soul, propitiating God by prayers, ceremonies, sacrifices etc."[14] He rejected Hinduism and accepted Buddhism. Hinduism is based on Vedas, Smritis, Puranas and Customs, which profess inequality, untouchability, casteism, unreasonable and unscientific beliefs and superstitions. Hinduism propounds religious determinism. Any thought, belief and action which contradicts Brahmanism would be subjected to punishment according to Manusmriti rules. Thus, the whole system went against the social philosophy of liberty, equality and fraternity. The worst sufferers of Hindu philosophy were the so-called Untouchables, Tribals and Backward Castes in proportion to their social status.

Dr. Babasaheb Ambedkar being born in an untouchable Mahar Community had to suffer a lot. In his school days, he was not allowed to take water to quench his thirst at a common watering place.[15] He was not allowed to learn sanskrit, which was presumably the language of the Gods.[16] However, he could continue his education in spite of several odds and obstacles in his way, only because of the new atmosphere created by British and Indian reformers. He completed his higher education in the famous Colombia University, New York and the London School of Economics and Politics and the Gray's Inn. He started his mission of emancipation of the untouchable and depressed classes in India from 1919 onwards.

Dr. Babasaheb Ambedkar launched a huge and unique *satyagraha* on 20th March, 1927 at Chowdar Tank at Mahad (Maharashtra) for asserting the right to equality. However, the orthodox caste Hindus attacked the peacefully returning untouchables from the said Tank. Subsequently, on 25th December 1927 the Manusmriti, which denied right to equality was burnt. He launched the famous *Satyagraha* for Temple entry at Kala Ram Temple at Nasik on 2nd March 1930, which intermittantly continued for almost five years, but in vain. Ultimately, he declared at Yeola (Nasik) on 13th October 1935 that he would renounce Hinduism based on Caste and Untouchability.

In his speech delivered in the Mahar Conference held under the presidentship of Rao Bahadur B.S.Venkatrao (Hyderabad) at Bombay on 31st May, 1936, he exhorted his brethren that, "religion is for man and not man for religion. If you want to organise yourself, change your religion. If you want to gain self-respect change your religion. If you want to create a society which ensures co-operation, and brotherhood change your religion. If you want to achieve power, change your religion. If you want equality change your religion. If you want independence, change your religion. If you want to make the world in which you live happily, change your religion."

"Why do you want to remain bound to a religion which does not even treat you as a human being ? Why do you remain in a religion which prohibits you from entering its temples? Why do you remain under that religion which prohibits you from drawing water from public wells? Why do you remain in that religion which bars you from decent occupations and jobs? Why do you remain in the religion which insults you at every step? The religion which teaches man to behave with man in an inhuman manner is not religion but infamy. The religion which does not recognise a human being as a human being is curse. The religion in which the touch of animals is permitted but the touch of a human being pollutes, is not a religion but the mockery of a religion. The religion which precludes some classes from education, forbids them to accumulate wealth and to bear arms, is not a religion but tyranny. The religion which compels the ignorant to remain ignorant and the poor to remain poor does not deserve to be called a religion."[17] This speech amply reveals the thought of Dr. Babasaheb Ambedkar on oppressive Hinduism in particular and the intrinsic philosophy of religion in general.

Although he declared to renounce Hinduism, but the question was which religion he should embrace. He thought that, the religion which fulfils certain tests of a true religion would be better. Those tests were:

(i) It should be based on morality;

(ii) It must be in accordance with science or reason;

(iii) It must recognize the fundamental tenets of liberty, equality and fraternity; and

(iv) It should not sanctify or ennoble poverty.[18]

He, however, thinks that it is the religion of Buddha or the Dhamma which could fulfil these requirements of a true religion. What is Dhamma is a pertinent question. According to Babasaheb Ambedkar the Dhamma is:

1. To maintain purity of body, purity of speech and purity of mind.
2. To live in Nibbana, which means release from passion or control over passion so as to enable one to walk on the path of righteousness.
3. To give up craving or greed for gain of exploitative possession.
4. To believe that all compound things are impermanent. "All things are produced by the combination of causes and conditions and have no idependent noumenon of their own, when the combination is dissolved, their destruction ensures."
5. To believe that *Karma* is the instrument of moral order. It is the *Karma Niyam* and not God which maintains the moral order in the universe.

The Buddha did not claim to be a God or a prophet or messenger of God. He was only a *Margadata*[19] and his Dhamma was merely a path of life.

The purpose of Religion is to explain the origin of the world. The purpose of Dhamma is to reconstruct the World".[20]

Following Buddha, Babasaheb Ambedkar admitted that, "Religion is necessary for a free society. Religion must relate to facts of life and not to theories and speculations about God, or Soul or Heaven or Earth." "The function of Religion is to reconstruct the world and to make it happy and not to explain its origin or its end." "Private ownership of property brings power to one class and sorrow to another." "All human beings are equal." "Worth and not birth is the measure of man." "Everyone has a right to learn. Learning is as necessary for man to live as food is." "Nothing is final". "Every thing is subject to the law of causation."[21]

Marx has not differentiated between a true religion and a false religion. He, however, made the blanket statement that religion is a opium of the people. "This charge is based upon the sermon on the Mount which is to be found in the Bible. The sermon on the Mount Sublimates poverty and weakness. It promises heaven to the poor and the weak. There is no sermon on the Mount to be found in the Buddha's teachings. His teachings is to acquire wealth lawfully."[22] Therefore, according to him, the 'charge' levelled by Marxists against the religion in general is not applicable to Buddhism, as such it is irrelevant.

Dr. Babasaheb Ambedkar, however rejects the orthodox and oppressive religion, but accepts that religion which is based on liberty equality and fraternity, rational thinking and human well-being. He agreed with Edmund Burke, who said that "True religion is the foundation of Society, the basis on which all true civil Government rests, and is also its sanction."[23] Eventually, he embraced Buddhism on 14th October 1956 on *Vijayadashami* at Nagpur and gave it to his millions of brethren.

It is also necessary to remember that he discerned the true Principles from the traditional Buddhism. He brought out the original creed by calling it, 'Dhamma' and not 'Dharma or religion. He gave the title *'Buddha and his*

Dhamma' to his magnum opus published posthumously. He thinks Siddharth Goutam Buddha was a human being subject to all attributes of human being like birth, growth, marriage, sufferings and sorrows, old age and death. He rejected the belief that he left the Palace in search of Truth after having seen a old man, dead body etc., and gave an conceivable reasoning of his *Pravarja*. He defined 'suffering' in its proper perspective, including the economic suffering. He gave proper interpretation to rebirth, *Karma* and non-violence and defined the duties of *Bhikkhus*. He did not want to create a dogmatic and indolent priest-class accepting obeisance from the laymen and merely blessing them. He thought that the Bhikkhu ought to be "The torch bearer of the Buddha's Ideal Society."[24] He studied Buddhist canonical literature keenly and arduously and found the True principles in a compendium. This implies that he believed in a social, scientific and moral way of life.

Buddha did not believe in any super-natural, inconceivable, unreasonable and illogical things, concepts or dogmas. He did not believe in God. He said very categorically that, "The question is did the Blessed Lord accept God as the creator of the Universe. The answer is "No". He did not. There are various grounds, why he rejected the doctrine of the existence of God.

Nobody has seen God. People only speak of God.

Nobody can prove that God has created the world. The world has evolved and is not created.

He argued that the doctrine of the existence of God is not based on Truth.

Who has seen Brahma face to face ?

"Nobody indeed," Goutama.

Is this not a case, ... of a man falling in love with a woman who he has not seen ? Yes, it is."

"...... if God is good then why do men become murderers, thieves, unchaste, liars, slanderers, abusive babblers, covetous, malicious and perverse ?"

"If there is a Supreme Creator, who is just and merciful, why then does so much injustice prevail in the world?"

"According to him the centre of religion lay not in the relation of man to God. It lay in the relation between man and man. The purpose of religion is to teach man, how he should behave towards other men so that all may be happy."

If there is not God (*Paramatma*) how there could be soul (or *Atma*) ?

If there is no Soul or *Atma*, how there could be 'rebirth' and of what ?

Dr. Babasaheb Ambedkar explains the theory of Dependent origination or *Pratit Samutpada* given by the Buddha himself in explanation the problem of creation of the world. He states that, "Did God Creat something out of nothing or did he create something out of something? It is impossible to believe that something could have been created out of nothing. If the so-called God has created something out of something, then that something out of which something new was crated has been in existence before he created anything. God cannot therefore be called the creator of that something which has existed before him. If something has been created by somebody out of something before God created anything then God cannot be said to be the creator or the first cause."[25]

The Buddha's Theory of Dependent origination *(Pratitya Samutpada)* precisely explains that several causes give birth to one effect. Cause and effect are interrelated. It is imperative to search the causes within material objects and not beyond that. Nothing is eternal, permanent and absolute. Buddha said that everything is transitory, non-permanent, relative and subject to conditions.

In the words of Y. Balaramamoorty, the Law of Dependence or Pratit Samutpada is, "That being thus this comes to be. From the coming to be of that, this arises. That being absent, this does not happen. From the cessation of that this ceases."

"This Law of Dependent origination is the core of Buddhist philosophy. Nothing exists by itself, nothing is absolute. Everything depends on something else. Everything is the effect of some cause. As long as the cause exists, effect also exists. When the cause ceases to be, the effect also vanishes. Everything is relative. Cause and effect are interrelated. One thing flows from the other."[26]

According to Budha, "a Sentient Being is a compound thing consisting of certain physical elements and certain mental elements. They are called *Khandas*."

The *Rupa Khanda* primarily consists of the physical elements such as earth, water, fire and air. They constitute the Body or *Rupa*.

Besides *Rupa Khanda*, there is such a thing as *Nama Khanda* which goes to make up a sentient Being. This *Nama Khanda* is called *Vinana*, or Consciousness.

Consiousness is result of the combination of the four elements, *Prithvi*, *Apa*, *Tej* and *Vayu*.

Those who object to this theory ask, "How is consciousness produced?"

"It is true that consciousness arises with birth and dies with death. What the Buddha said was that wherever there was *Rupa* or *Kaya* there was consciousness accompanying it. To give an analogy from science, there is an electric field and whenever there is an electric field it is always accompanied by a magnetic field. No one knows how the magnetic field is created or how it arises. But it always exists alongwith the electric field. Why should not the same relationship be said to exist between body and consciousness?".

"All functions assigned to the soul are performed by consciousness. A soul without any function is an absurdity. This is how the Buddha disproved the existence of the soul."[27]

In his scientific analysis and interpretation of Buddhism, he applied three tests, first "Buddha was nothing, if not rational, if not logical; second anything attributed to the Buddha which did not relate to man's welfare can not be accepted to be the word of Buddha; third, Buddha divides all matters into two classes, one, about which he was certain and about which he was not certain. Regarding first, he expressed his views in definite terms, but regarding second, he gives only tentative views. Thus, he found out True Buddhism.[28]

Conclusion

Karl Marx and Babasaheb Ambedkar did not believe in religion, God and such abstract ideas having no rational explanation. They thought that religion is the creation of priestly class and feudal class for their selfish ends. It is an instrument to keep the masses in ignorance and protect the vested interests of the exploitative ruling class. However, Babasaheb Ambedkar discarding unscientific Hindu religion believed in rational Buddhism as a way of life. His Dhamma is quite old in its foundation, but modern in reality. He preached love, compassion, non-violence and peace.

Dr. Babasaheb Ambedkar has tried to explain as to how a sentient being is a compound thing consisting of certain physical elements and certain mental elements. Karl Marx has not dealt with the matter to its logical conclusion, but contemplated that everything is reflextion of the matter. Thus, both of them had tried to co-relate 'cause and effect ' from philosophical and logical point of view. However, they were primarily concerned with the improvement of socio-economic condition of the oppressed class rather than finding the laws of nature. If not God, what, is a very complicated and incomprehensible question which could be better explained by the advancing science and technology and not by religion.

Notes and References

1. Encyclopaedia of Social Sciences.
2. Encyclopaedia of Religions quoted by Broom and Salznick is Sociology p. 400.
   Muruzen Co.Ltd., Kokyo.
3. Volkov Genrikh: *Birth of a Genius*: p. 75.
4. *Ibid.,* p. 77.

5. *Ibid.,* p. 78.
6. *Ibid.,* p. 79.
7. Sdobnikov Yuri: Karl Marx; A Biography, p. 31.
8. *Ibid.,* p. 31.

8(a) For details see Franz Mehring's Book, "Karl Marx", pp. 72-73 (1948).

9. Marx Karl: Collected Works, p. 175.
10. *Ibid.,* p. 10.
11. Karl-Marx *"Contribution to the Critique of Hegel's Philosophy of Law"* in: Karl Marx, Frederick Engels, Collected Works, Vol. III. p. 175.
12. Barmenkov A. Freedom of Conscience in the USSR. pp. 12-13.
13. *Ibid.,* p. 13.
14. DBAWS Vol. II. p. 316.
15. Keer Dhananjay: Dr. Ambedkar : Life and Mission, p. 13. Popular Prakashan, Bombay (1971).
16. *Ibid.,* p. 18.
17. Das Bhagwan: *Thus Spoke Ambedkar*, Vol. IV, pp. 61-62. Ambedkar Sahitya Prakashana.
    West of Chord Rtd., IInd Stage, Rajaji Nagar, Bangalore, (1979)
18. Ahir D.C. (Ed.) Dr. Ambedkar on Buddhism, pp. 26-27. Siddharth Publication, People's Education Society, Anand Bhavan, Fort, Mumbai. (1982)
19. DBAWS.Vol. II. p. 218.
20. *Ibid.,* p. 322.
21. DBAWS.Vol. III, p. 442, (1987).
22. *Ibid.,* p. 460.
23. *Ibid.,* Vol. I. p.76.
24. *Ibid.,* Vol. II, p. 434.
25. *Ibid.,* pp. 251, 252, 254, 255
26. Sankrityayan Rahul: (Ed) Buddhism: The Marxist Approach, p. 38.
27. DBAWS Vol. II, pp. 262, 263, 264.
28. The Buddha and His Dhamma, (2nd) Preface by R.R. Bhole, (1973).

6

Thoughts on State and Revolution

It is generally conceived that the state is the natural, universal, essential and eternal institution. According to Aristotle, "the state came into existence for the sake of life and state continues to exist for the sake of good life." Man being a social animal he lives in society. The society provides him certain amenities and protects his life from internal foes and external aggressions. Society has to be properly managed. The people formed the state by their own will for their own benefit. The state is an institution which equally needs everywhere. There is no place in the world where had been no state or where is no state. It is essential in the sense it maintains peace and order in the society, maintains civil and political rights and protects them in the event of foreign aggression. It has in continuation from the time immemorial and still it is in existence as before.

(A) Karl Marx on State

1. Karl Marx, however did not believe in the state as an essential, eternal and inevitable institution. In the primitive society, according to Karl Marx, there was no state. However, when the human society was divided into two classes, it became essential for the bourgeoisie class to have the state with armed forces to protect the privileged classes. In the opinion of Karl Marx, state is the instrument of exploitation of the proletariat, as such it needs to be destroyed.

In the words of Mandel "the state is a special organ that appears at a certain moment in the historical evolution of mankind, and that is condemned to disappear in the course of this same evolution. It is born from the division of society into classes and will disappear at the same time this division disappears. It is born as an instrument in the hands of the possessing class for the purpose of maintaining the domination of this class over society and it will disappear alongwith this class domination."[1]

According to Marxist Theory "the state is, by definition, a group of men who exercise the functions that in the beginning were exercised by all members of the collectivity. These men contribute no productive labour but are supported by the other members of society."[2]

The Parliament is "to serve as a common meeting place where the collective interests of the bourgeois could be formulated." "Thus, capitalists power is concentrated outside Parliament and outside the institutions born of universal suffrage."[3] Later on the right of administration of justice became a monopoly of a minority dominated by the feudal Lords.

The Bourgeoisie society is based on Bourgeoisie state. There existed the capitalist class and priestly class. The whole administrative machinery is manned and controlled by the Bourgeoisie state power. The proletariat class is deprived of the pursuit of pleasure, rights and privileges. They remain alive on sale of their labour to the capitalists and ultimately lead their life in poverty and deprivation. All the means of productions are owned and controlled by the capitalists, even they purchase and own the labour.

The proletariat class includes the workers and labourers who get marginal wages for their livelihood. They are, of course in majority. However, they are under the hegemonic power of the capitalists and priestly class. They would get liberation after the communistic revolution, and after establishing dictatorship of the proletariat. However, the dictatorship of the majority proletariat would be the real democracy of the majority in the Communistic Society.

According to the Communist Theory, the state is but an instrument of exploitation. The dominant class provides its philosophy and necessary succour to the government machinery and all social, political, legal, economic and educational institutions so that all the institutions or organs of the society would develop vested interests and would exploit every possible opportunity for mutual benefit.

The communists think that the state exists only to protect the interests of the capitalists or Bourgeoisie class. It was never in the interests of the proletariat, and it would not be in the interests of the common people. It is viewed as a product of class-antagonism and it would continue in existence till the class-antagonism, remains in existence.

According to Marxist Theory, the state did not exist for all the time. The state appears to the extent that society is divided into classes; and it would disappear alongwith the disappearance of social divisions in the society.

The most characteristic features of this state machinery are two institutions: 'The bureacracy and the standing army, which are a "parasite" on the body of bourgeoisie society a parasite created by the internal antagonisms which rend that society, but a parasite which "chokes" all its vital pores."[4]

Another characteristic feature of the state is force. In the words of Lenin, "the state is a special organisation of force: It is an organisation of violence for the suppression of some class. The exploiting classes need political rule to maintain exploitation, i.e., in the selfish interests of an insignificant minority against the vast majority of the people. The exploited classes need political rule in order to completely abolish all exploitation i.e., in the interests of the vast majority of the people, and against the insignificant minority consisting of the modern slave-owners—the land owners and capitalists."[5]

[2] Karl Marx on Revolution

Karl Marx thought that the revolution is inevitable

outcome of the class-struggle. He said that the revolution would develop in two phases. "In the first, the bourgeoisie would be engaged in a struggle with Feudalism as represented by absolute monarchy and its various survivals. In this struggle, the proletariat must support the bourgeoisie and then look forward for an opportunity to capture power from the bourgeoisie. This alliance was to be merely tactical as there existed the fundamental antagonism between the bourgeoisie and proletariat. In the second phase of the revolution, the bourgeois which destroyed feudalism, would itself be destroyed by the proletariat in alliance with left wing bourgeoisie elements, which would be later on discarded by the proletariat."[6]

According to Marx, the revolution is inevitale; for the transition of power from the bourgeoisie to the proletariat. "They expect that blood may be shed, lives may be lost. But, they ask, what is the alternative? Is the alternative to the loss of life that may accompany the socialist revolution, no suffering, no blood shed, no violence, no loss of life ? Not at all. The alternative is much greater suffering more blood-shed, more violence, more loss of life in capitalists wars."[7]

Eventually, Marx openly declars that, "their ends can be attained by the forcible overthrow of all existing social conditions. Let the ruling classes tremble at a communistic revolution. Proletarians have nothing to lose but their chains. They have a world to win. Workingmen of all countries unite!"[8] "The revolutions are not made by laws" further, he states, that, "force is the mid-wife of every old society preg-nant with a new one. It is, itself an economic power."[9]

"Revolution is, "in the words of Huberman and Sweezy, "not merely a shift in the personnel of the government from one member of the ruling class to another, as the result of a rebellion or insurrection. For Marxists the term "revolution" has a much more profound meaning. It is the transference of economic and political power from one class to another class. The kind of revolution that Marx advocated, the socialist revolution, means specifically the transfer of power from the capitalist class to the working class; it means revising the relations between the working class and the capitalist so that the working class becomes the ruling class; it means the destruction of capitalism through the socialisation of the means of production."

"The seizure of Political Power by the working class is the first step in the revolution. The second step is to recast the social order and to crush the resistance of the capitalist class to the change."[10] Jaiprakash Narayan has rightly said that, "Marxism is a science of society and a scientific method of social change that includes social revolution. As such there can be no room for dogmatism or fundamentalism in Marxist thought. Who on the one hand call Marxism Scientific and on the other introduce dogmatism into it do it great disservice. In science there is no such thing as final truth."[10(a)]

Rao Saheb Kasabe states that Marx favoured not merely political revolution, but that revolution which would culminate into social revolution. Hence, he condemns the Jacobian Terrorists who thought to capture power by swords.[10(b)]

In between the Proletarian revolution and classless society, there shall be the interim period or a period of transition, in which the state has to be retained. The state in this period would be "revolutionary dictatorship of the proletariat." During this period the "Bourgeois Law" is not abolished in its entirety till socialism is fully consolidated.

According to Marx, "The working class, in the course of development, will substitute for the old bourgeoisie society an association which will preclude classes and their antagonism, and there will be no more political power proper, since political power is precisely the official expression of class antagonism in bourgeois society."[11]

[3] Dictatorship of The Proletariat

Nature and characteristics of the proletarian state could be described as under:

" The proletarian state is at one and the same time, a

state and not a state. It becomes less and less a state. It is a state that begins to witheraway at the very moment it is born, as Marx and Lenin correctly said. Marx developing the theory of the proletarian state, of the dictatorship of the proletariat, as he called it, the state that withers away, gave it several characteristics, examples of which were found in the Paris Commune of 1871. There are three essential characteristics:

1. *No distinct separation between the executive and legislative powers:* "Bodies are needed which enact laws and at the same time enforce them. In short, it is necessary to revert to the state that was born of the primitive communism of the clan and the tribe and that can still found in the ancient Athenian popular assembly." "The deliberative assemblies must have real executive power at their disposal."[11(a)]

2. *Public Offices to be elective, to the greatest extent*: "It is not only members of the deliberative assemblies, who should be elected. Judges, high level functionaries, officers of the militia, supervisors of education, managers of public works should also be elected."

   "In the proletarian state this electing of Public Officials must be accompanied in all cases by the right of recall i.e., voting unsatisfactory officials out of office at any time."[12]

3. *No excessive salaries*: "No official, no member of representative and legislative bodies, no individual exercising a state power, should receive a salary higher than that of a skilled worker. That is the only valid method of preventing people from seeking public office as a way of feathering their nests and sponging on society, the only valid way to get rid of the career-hunters and parasites known to all previous societies."[13]

   "The direct antithesis to the empire was the commune." It was the "specific form" of "a republic that was not only to remove the monarchical form of class rule, but class-rule itself."[14]

   "The Commune was formed of the municipal

councillors, chosen by universal suffrage in the various wards of Paris, responsible and revocable at any time. The majority of its members were naturally workingmen, or acknowledged representatives of the working class. The police which until then had been the instrument of the government, was at once stripped of its political attributes, and turned into the responsible and at all times revocable instrument of the Commune. So were the officials of all other branches of the administration. From the members of the commune downwards, public service had to be done at workmen's wages. The privileges and the representation allowances of the high dignitaries of state disappeared alongwith the dignitaries themselves. Having once got rid of the standing army and the police, the instruments of the physical force of the old government, the Commune proceeded at once to break the instrument of spiritual suppression, the power of the priests... The judicial functionaries lost that sham independence.... They were thenceforward to be elective responsible, and revocable..."[15]

Thus, in the words of Lenin, "the Commune is the first attempt by a Proletarian revolution to smash the bourgeois state machine; and it is the political form, "at last discovered", by which the smashed state machine can and must be replaced."[16] After the smashing of the state and establishing a classless society, there would be period of transition. During the transition period the Communist theory contemplates to establish the dictatorship of the Proletariat. During this period the state is not abolished, but it withers away. The expression "The State withers away" is very well chosen, for it indicates both the gradual and the spontaneous nature of the process."[17] During this period of transition the dictatorship of the Proletariat will establish real democracy for the people. During transition suppression of the exploiting minority by the exploited majority is still necessary; the state is still necessary, but this is now a 'transitional state'. The people can suppress the exploiters even with a very simple machine or almost without "machine", "by the simple organisation of the armed people."[18]

"Thus, the society having attained equality of all the classes and having established a real Communist State, they would be ruled by the Principle—"from each according to his ability, to each according to his needs," i.e., when people have become so accustomed to observing the fundamental rules of social intercourse and when their labour has become so productive that they will voluntarily work according to their ability."[19]

[B] Babasaheb Ambedkar on State

1. Dr. Babasaheb Ambedkar obviously believes in state as a machinery to bring about welfare of the people. He thinks that the state is a means to achieve an end of well being of the people; without which life would not only be miserable, but virtually impossible and inconceivable. Of all the organisations, the state is a supreme and primordial organisation, legally empowered to control and co-ordinate various aspects of social life. It protects life, liberty and property of the people.

   The government is one of the essential elements of the state. It is like a head of the family, a managing committee which manages affairs of a company or organisation and manages the affairs of the state.

   There are several forms of government, such as monarchy, aristocracy, democracy, dictatorship etc., Dr. Babasaheb Ambedkar had indomitable faith in Parliamentary democracy as the best form of government and the best protector of the liberty. He believed that, "Law and order is the medicine of the body politic, and when the body politic goes sick this medicine must be administered."[20] The state is to protect the state from external aggression.

While putting forth his argument in the Round Table Conference, London he said that "we must have a government, in which the men in power will give their undivided allegiance to the best interest of the country. We must have a government in which men in power, knowing where obedience will end and resistance will begin, will not be afraid to amend the social and economic code of life which the dictates of justice and expediency so urgently call for."[21]

He was quite aware of caste character and red-tapism of the administrative machinery. It owes its duty firstly to higher castes and vested interests. It was quite indifferent to the welfare of the people of the weaker sections. Therefore, he said very categorically that, "the Scheduled Castes had no fear of bad laws being made to their prejudice. What they had to fear about was bad administration. This bad administration was due to the absence of men belonging to the Scheduled Castes in the administration."[22] Therefore, he thought that the administrative machinery should be reformed and made representative of all castes, communities or interests, so that every needy person would be able to get justice.

He bestows the responsibility of maintaining internal security, peace and order and external security from external aggression on the state. He bestows the responsibility of maintaining and protecting fundamental rights of the people and implementing socialistic programme contemplated under the directive principles of state policy.

He was neither an anarchist nor a partisan of dictatorship of proletariat; but he invigorates the state to fulfil its obligation by undertaking welfare activities for the benefit of the people. In a democratic society, the state assumes the role of responsible government as an apparatus of social change and well-being of the people. When that apparatus works for a few at the cost of others, the people have the voting power so that they are empowered to give a befitting lesson in the election. Thus, the government could be changed by democratic method and not by revolution. The government may be changed and not the state. The state is under obligation to fulfil its constitutional responsibility, "to plan the economic life of the people on lines which would lead to highest point of productivity without closing every avenue to private enterprises and also provide for the equitable distribution of wealth."[23]

[2] Constitutional Means

Dr. Babasaheb Ambedkar was a true follower of Lord Buddha. Saint Kabir and Mahatma Phule and was brought up in the liberal tradition of America and England. Therefore he believes in Law and Constitution as instruments of socio-economic change. He rightly thought that law can not be static or rigid. Its roots are in democracy. He exhorted that, "The True Function of Law consists in repairing the faults of the society."[24] While stating the true nature of his struggle, he states that, "Our struggle is for freedom. It is a battle for the reclamation of human personality which has been suppressed and mutilated by the Hindu Social System."[25] He said following Burke that, "the use of force alone is but temporary. It may subdue for a moment, but it does not remove the subduing again."[26] His whole struggle was for justice, and it was based on just means.

However, while declaring his resolve to launch the *Satyagraha* at Mahad Chowder Tank on September 11, 1927 at Damodar Hall, Bombay, Babasaheb Ambedkar said that "fight, whether violent or non-violent, was just if the end sought was good. If the end sought was just, the insistence on its achievement and the fight for it must be equally just....." If wounding one's feelings is violence, he said, "Gandhi's *Satyagraha* is also based on violence." "Truly speaking," he concluded, "the law should be non-violence wherever possible; violence whenever necessary."[27]

While addressing the conference of the Samata Sainik Dal, on 19th July 1942 at Nagpur he said that "he had love for the principle of non-violence, but he differentiated non-violence from abject surrender. He told the volanteers that it did not benefit a man to live a life of surrender, servitude and helplessness. He declared that he believed with the Saint Tukaram that destruction of the wicked was also a form of non-violence. Although love and kindness towards all creatures was a part of the principle of non-violence to destroy all evil doers was the principal element in the doctrine of *ahimsa.* Without that, *ahimsa* was an empty shell, a beatitude. *Shakti* (Strength) and *Shila* (Character) should be their ideal."[28]

While presenting the Constitution to the nation, on 25th November, 1949 he gave a caution to the People of India, that, "we must abandon the bloody methods of revolution. It means that we must abandon the method of civil-disobedience, non-co-operation and *Satyagraha.* When there was no way left for constitutional methods for achieving economic and social objectives, there was a great deal of justification for unconstitutional methods. But where constitutional methods are open, there can be no justification for these unconstitutional methods. These methods are nothing but the Grammar of Anarchy and the sooner they are abandoned, the better for us."[29]

Following Buddha he said we wage war for "Lofty virtues for right endeavour, for sublime wisdom—for these, things do we wage war: therefore, we are called warriors. Where virtue is in danger do not avoid fighting, do not be mealy-mouthed."[30] Thus, he permits "war" when there is need to protect virtues. However, he gave more emphasis on cultivating the mind with virtue. He thought that mind is the origin of all actions good or bad; as such mind should be cultivated in good thought. It is necessary to restrain one's mind so that it would detract from passion, lusts and evils. What do these statements indicate? They need to be properly construed. Ideas in favour of non-violence and constitutional means seem to be dominating over the ideas of violence. He stood throughout his life for non-violence and constitutional means.

It seems that Dr. Babasaheb Ambedkar contemplates to undertake social reforms as a necessary pre-condition before the economic or political reforms. He thinks that a pre-revolution was necessary before the revolution in a society dominated by the caste and creed considerations. He states, "History bears out the Proposition that political revolutions have always been preceded by social and religious revolutions. The religious reformation started by Luther was the precursor of the political emancipation of the European People. In England puritanism led to the establishment of political liberty. Puritanism founded the new world. It was puritanism which won the war of American Independence and Puritanism was a religious movement. The same is true of the Muslim Empire. Before the Arabs became a political power they had undergone a thorough religious revolution started by the Prophet Mohammad. Even Indian History supports the same conclusion. The political revolution, led by Chandragupta was preceded by the religious and social revolution of Buddha. The political revolution, led by Shivaji was preceded by the religious and social reform brought about by the saints of Maharashtra. The political revolution of the Skikhs was preceded by the religious and social revolution, led by Guru Nanak. It is unnecessary to add more illustrations. These will suffice to show that the emancipation of the mind and the soul is a necessary preliminary for the political expansion of the people."[31]

Dr. Babasaheb Ambedkar said in very unequivocal terms that, "one may contend that economic motive is not the only motive by which man is actuated. That economic power is the only kind of power no student of human society can accept. That social status of an individual by itself often becomes a source of power and authority is made clear by the sway which the Mahatmas, have held over the common man. Why do millionaires in India obey penniless Sadhus and Fakirs? Why do millions of paupers in India sell their Triffling Trinckets which constitute their only wealth and go to Benaras or Mecca ?[32] Religion, social status and property are all sources of power and authority."[33] All these elements constituted the steel frame of society which he determined to smash it.

He was very much clear about the success or failure of the prospective socialist revolution in India. He stated that, "the economic reform contemplated by the socialists can not come about unless there is a revolution resulting in the seizure of power. That seizure of power must be by a Proletariat. The first question I ask is: will the Proletariat of India combine to bring about this revolution? What will move men to such an action? It seems to me that other things being equal the only thing that will move one man to take such an action is the feeling that other man with whom he is acting are actuated by feeling of equality and fraternity and above all of justice. Men will not join in a revolution for the equalisation of property unless they know that after the revolution is achieved they will be treated equally and there will be no discrimination of caste and creed. The assurance of a socialist leading the revolution that he does not believe in caste, I am sure, will not suffice. The assurance must be the assurance proceeding from much deeper foundation, namely, the mental attitude of the compatriots towards one another in their spirit of personal equality and fraternity. Can it be said that the proletariat of India poor as it is recognise no distinctions except that of the rich and the poor ? Can it be said that the poor in India recognise no such distinctions of caste or creed, high or low? If the fact is that they do, what unity of front can be expected from such a proletariat in its action against the rich? How can there be a revolution if the proletariat can not present a united front?.... I can not see how a socialist state in India can function for a second without having to grapple with the problems created by the prejudices which make Indian people observe the distinction of high and low, clean and unclean."[34]

In the words of M.P. Mangudkar, Karl Marx painted "a somewhat romantic picture of the industrial proletariat. Marx said that the industrial proletariat is the vanguard of total revolution. Dr. Ambedkar challenged this concept. He said that this concept has no relevance to Indian society. Industrial workers are divided into various Castes and Caste-Hindu workers, who do not like to touch the untouchable industrial workers. The caste system has created great divisions amongst the industrial workers themselves. Under such conditions how can the industrial workers be united ?"[35]

It would be worthwhile to revive the plan of alliance of industrial labour, agricultural labour and other labourers into one united front or party as done by Dr. Babasaheb Ambedkar under the banner of Independent Labour Party (1936). Even for this purpose, it is necessary to bring about socio-political consciousness among the labour class. Probably, the capitalist and Brahmanic forces would try to foil the plan of the labour class. It is, however necessary to work unitedly alongwith the right thinking elites in the society and bring about a new awareness. If this plan becomes, successful it would be a real and sustainable plan.

[3] Faith in Democracy

Dr. Babasaheb Ambedkar had indomitable faith in democracy. He believes that dictatorship is dictatorship, whether it is by proletariat or capitalists. He had staunch faith in the trinity of liberty, equality and fraternity. He does not want to sacrifice one principle for another. He thought that democracy stands for peaceful change and development. It is based on consent of the people. Every citizen has equal share in the decision-making process. Therefore, it aims at welfare of the people at large.

He defines democracy as, "a form and a method of government whereby revolutionary changes in the economic and social life of the people are brought about without bloodshed."[36] When decisions are taken by majority and corrupt government could be toppled down by majority, elections are held by adult franchise and rules are framed by majority vote, where is the need of bloody revolution in such a society. Every difference of opinion be communicated properly and adjusted properly through understanding and negotiations.

He states that political democracy rests on four premises. They are:–

1. The individual is an end in himself.
2. The individual has certain inalienable rights which must be guaranteed to him by the Constitution.
3. The individual shall not be required to relinguish any of his constitutional rights as a price of any privilege.
4. The state shall not delegate power to private persons to govern others.[37]

All these points are self-explanatory. The main objective of a democratic government is the welfare of the individuals.

He, however states that political democracy can not be successful unless there is social and economic democracy at its base. The society must be free from conflicting social groups, economic groups and communal groups. He states that there ought to be caste less and classless society for the successful working of democracy.

Therefore, he thought to base his ideal society on liberty, equality, fraternity and justice. For achieving economic equality he proposes 'state-socialism.'

He was, however aware of the fact that in India there is communal majority instead of political majority. In such an orthodox society, public opinion is always dominated by the priestly class and the capitalist class. Therefore, he proposed to have "non-parliamentary government," wherein the effect of caste and communal majority could be overcome.

He prescribes certain conditions which are necessary for the successful working a democracy. They are: (1) Equality (2) Two party system (3) Equality in law, and administration (4) Constitutional morality (5) No Tyranny of majority, and (6) moral order and public conscience.

Thus, he stands for democracy and thinks to make it successful as a need of modern society.

Conclusion

So far as ideas regarding the state and revolution are concerned Karl Marx and Babasaheb Ambedkar differ in their thoughts and approaches. Marx thought to smash the Bourgioisie state but did not give a definite plan as to what would take its place after it has been smashed. He states that so long the antagonistic forces in the society will remain, the state will remain in existence. As soon as those forces come to an end, the state will wither away. In Soviet Russia the state did not wither away. Now, it has been rejuveneted. His plan of destroying the state by 'forcible overthrow' or by bloody revolution cannot be a final solution.

According Dr. Babasaheb Ambedkar the state is inevitable to protect the people from internal dissensions and external invasions. It is also necessary to bring state-socialism into reality. The government which represents the state ought to be representative, responsive and responsible to the people. He said that for bringing about any change in the society constitutional means ought to be applied.

Both the thinkers differ on the vital issue of nature of government. Karl Marx advocates for dictatorship of the proletariat, though for undefined time; and Babasaheb Ambedkar stands for democracy. He could secure all the lost rights and privileges to the Depressed Classes by peaceful struggle and a unique strategy. It was but a great revolution!

Notes and References

1. Desai A.R. (Ed): The Marxist Theory of the State, pp. 26-27.
   Shah Memorial Trust, Jaykutir, Taikalwadi Rtd. Bombay (1979)
2. *Ibid.,* p. 35.
3. *Ibid.,* p. 32.
4. Lenin: *The State and Revolution*, p. 31.
   Progress Publishers, Moscow, (Edition, 1977)
5. *Ibid.,* p. 26-27.
6. Sharma R.P. Modern Western Political Thoguht, p. 368.
   Sterling Publishers Pvt.Ltd.,New Delhi. (Edn. 1976).
7. Huberman and Sweezy: *Introduction to Socialism*, p. 77.
   Progressive Book Depot; New Delhi. (Edn. 1979).
8. Marx-Engels: *Manifesto of the Communist Party*, p. 96.
9. Marx Karl: Capital. Vol. I. p. 776.
   by Dona Torr. George Allen & Unwin Ltd. London, (1949).
10. Huberman and Sweezy: *Introduction to Socialism*, p. 77.

10(a) Prasad Bimla (Ed) Socialism Sarvodaya and Democracy p. 41.
Asia Publishing House, Bombay, (1964).

10(b) Kasabe Raosaheb: *Ambedkar Ani Marx*, p. 326.
Sugava Prakashan Pune, (Edn. 2006).

11. Marx Karl: *The Poverty of Philosophy*, p. 151.

11(a) Desai A.R. *The Marxist Theory of the State*, pp. 44-45.

12. *Ibid.,* p. 45.
13. *Ibid.,* p. 45.
14. Lenin: *The State and Revolution*, p. 42.
15. *Ibid.,* p. 42.
16. *Ibid.,* p. 55.
17. *Ibid.,* p. 85.

18. *Ibid.,* p. 86.
19. *Ibid.,* p. 92.
20. DBAWS: Vol.I, p. 359 (1979).
21. DBAWS: Vol. II, p. 505 (1982).
22. Das Bhagwan: *Thus Spoke Ambedkar*: Vol. I. p. 85. Bheem Patrika, Jullundur (3rd 1977)
23. DBAWS: Vol.I: p. 408.
24. Das Bhagwan: Thus Spoke Ambedkar: Vol. III, p. 191.
25. Ibid., p. 137.
26. DBAWS: Vol.13. p. 13.
27. Keer Dhananjay: Dr. Ambedkar: Life and Mission, p. 90-91.
28. *Ibid.,* p. 352-352.
29. DBAWS: Vol. 13. p. 1215.
30. DBAWS: Vol. 11. p. 447.
31. DBAWS: Vol. 1. pp. 43-44.
32. *Ibid.,* p. 44.
33. *Ibid.,* p. 45.
34. *Ibid.,* pp. 46-47.
35. An article by M.P. Mangudkar, in Dr. B.R. Ambedkar, Edited by K.N. Kadam. p. 168.
36. Ambedkar B.R.Conditions precedent for the successful working of Democracy, p. 3.
    Publisher by Smt. Panchbhai, Buddha, Nagar, Nagpur.
37. For details, see: DBAWS. Vol. I. p. 409.

7

Thoughts on Socialism

In the modern period the term *'socialist'* was firstly used in England in 1827 to denote a person who discarded the Laissez-faire policy. The genesis of *'socialism'* could be attributed to glaring economic inequalities caused by the Laissez-faire policy at the one hand and the unflinching urge of the people to abandone it for deriving the fullest benefit of 'liberty, equality and fraternity', coined during the French Revolution at the other. In the words of Frederick Watkins, "socialism arose out of the failure of liberalism to live upto its own optimistic promises of economic welfare. Only the relatively rich and enterprising were in a position to take full advantage of the new economic order. This was a bitter disappointment to the humanitarian hopes of those who had embraced liberalism in the expectation that the benefits of economic progress would be shared by all mankind. Socialism arose as a response to their disappointment."[1]

Subsequently, several thinkers came forward to draw an outline of the ideology of socialism in their own way. Prominent among them were Saint Simon (1760-1825), Charles Fourier (1772-1837), Robert Owen (1771-1858), and many others. Karl Marx, however underestimates all the preceding theories of socialism branding them as 'utopian socialism', and advances his own, as "scientific socialism". In the words of Dr. Babasaheb Ambdkar, "Karl Marx is no doubt the father of modern socialism or communism but he was not interested merely in propounding the theory of socialism. That had been done long before him by others. Marx was more interested in proving that his socialism was scientific. His crusade was as much against the capitalists as it was against those whom he called the utopian socialists. He disliked them both. It is necessary to note this point because Marx attached the greatest importance to the scientific character of his socialism."[2]

Dr. Babasaheb Ambedkar also believes in Socialism. However, his socialism is called as 'State-socialism', which aims "to establish statesocialism without abrogating parlimentary democracy and without leaving its establishment to the will of a parliamentary democracy."[3] "It establishes state-socialism by the law of the Constitution and thus makes it unalterable by any act of the legislature and the executive."[4]

Before proceeding further it would be pertinent to know as to what is socialism.

According to New Encyclopaedia Britanica, "Socialism is a system of social organisation in which private property and the distribution of income are subject to social control rather than the determination by individuals pursuing their own interest or by the market forces of capital."[5]

According to the Random House Dictionary, Socialism is, "a theory or system of social organisation that advocates the ownership and control of industry, capital, land, etc., by the community as a whole."

In socialism the interests of the community are of primordial importance rather than individual interests. All the means of production including land, industries, capital, mines and other sources of production are generally owned by the community as a whole. Character of production is determined not by consideration of profit but by social needs.

The common man, especially the labour class is free from primary needs, as such he is expected to enjoy real freedom. Economic classes including labour classes and the capitalist classes would have cordial relations amongst them. They would forget class-consciousness and hence there would not be class-struggle

All the people would get equal opportunities to develop their personality as per their own ability and conscience. When there is equality, there will be liberty and fraternity among the people.

There would not be any privileged class accumulating money and acquiring political power at the cost of others.

During the time of drought or distress or exploitation of one class by other class, the community would act as guardian of the people and protect the interests of the people on priority basis.

The individual would not own private property. Therefore, there is no need to protect private property from usurpation by anybody. Therefore, the society would not feel the inevitability and necessity of the state. However, the government would properly plan to increase the production and standard of the people.

Karl Marx was, however not fully convinced with the prevailing ideologies of socialism. Therefore, he lumped them as the "utopians" and discarded them. Of the socialist thinkers Saint-Simon, "advocated a more or less centralised economy under state control." "Fourier's plan of model community or Phalanstery resembled' as an elaborate resort hotel". Proudhan 'hoped to setup a nationwide system of workers co-operatives'. Thus there was no common consensus and convincing utilitarian philosophy. Consequently, Marx was impelled to propound a new ideology with a new content and form for the benefit of the exploited masses; known as 'Scientific Socialism.'

Dr. Babasaheb Ambedkar also was not satisfied with the contemporary socialist ideas. Neither 'Scientific Socialism' nor Democratic Socialism, nor the Gandhian brand of socialism could appeal him to his conscience. His inner urge for social justice, rationalistic approach, classless and casteless society, constitutional means and high moral and material standard naturally impelled him to propound 'State-socialism'.

[A] Scientific Socialism

Karl Marx propounded scientific socialism. In his endeavour he was morally and materially supported by his friend and life-long companion Frederick Engels.

According to Karl-Marx, "the class-struggle between the Proletariat and bourgeoisie would eventually culminate into Proletarian revolution; in which the Proletariat would necessarily smash the bourgeoisie state and seize power from them."

While elaborating what kind of new social order will have to be Karl Marx stated in express words that, "In the first place it will inaugurate a democratice Constitution and thereby, directly or indirectly, the political rule of the proletariat." (Oct.1847)

Further, he stated that certain measures are to be followed. They are:

1. Limitation of private ownership by means of progressive taxation, high inheritance taxes, abolition of inheritance by collateral lines (brothers, nephews etc.) compulsory loans and so forth.
2. Gradual expropriation of landed proprietors, factory owners, railway and shipping magnates, partly through competition on the part of state industry and partly directly through compensation in assignations.
3. Confiscation of the property of all emigrants and rebels against the majority of the people.
4. Organisation of the labour or employment of the proletarians on national estates in national factories and workshops, thereby putting an end to competition among the workers themselves and compelling the factory-owners, as long as they still exist, to pay the same increased wages as the state.
5. Equal liability to work for all members of society until complete abolition of private ownership. Formation of industrial armies, especially for agriculture

6. Centralisation of the credit and banking systems in the hands of the state by means of a national bank with state capital and the suppression of all private banks and bankers.
7. Increase of national factories, workshops, railways and ships, cultivation of all uncultivated land and improvement of land already cultivated in the same proportion in which the capital and workers at the disposal of the nation increase.
8. Education of all children, as soon as they are old enough to do without the first maternal care, in national institutions and of the expense of the nation. Education combined with production.
9. The erection of large palaces on national estates as common dwelling for communities of citizens engaged in industry as well as agriculture and combining the advantages of both urban and rural life without the one-sidedness and disadvantages of either.
10. The demolition of all insanitory and badlybuilt dwelling and town districts.
11. Equal right of inheritance to be enjoyed by illegitimate and legitimate children.
12. Concentration of all means of Transport in the hands of the nation."[6]

This programme was given by Marx and Engels in October 1847. Again the same was reiterated in *Manifesto of the Communist Party,* in January 1848.

Later on, the Communist League, an international association of workers commissioned Karl Marx and Friedric Engels at the Congress held in London in November 1847 to draw up "a detailed theoretical and practical programme of the Communist Party." The Draft was approved by the Congress. It became the *Manifesto of the Comunist* Party. It was firstly published in English in 1850. The *Manifesto, inter alia,* bears the programme of the party for consolidation of socialist revolution. It was a mere reiteration and confirmation of the October 1947 measues. It was as under:

1. Abolition of property in land and application of all rents of land to public purposes.
2. A heavy progressive or graduated income tax.
3. Abolition of all right of inheritance.
4. Confiscation of the property of all emigrants and rebels.
5. Centralisation of credit in the hands of the state, by means of a national bank with state capital and an exclusive monopoly.
6. Centralisation of the means of communication and transport in the hands of the state.
7. Extension of factories and instruments of production owned by the state; the bringing into cultivation of waste-lands, and the improvement of the soil generally in accordance with a common plan.
8. Equal liability of all the labour. Establishment of industrial armies especially for agriculture.
9. Combination of agriculture with manufacturing industries; gradual abolition of the distinction between town and country, by a more equaitable distribution of the population over the country.
10. Free education for all children in Public Schools. Abolition of children's factory labour in its present form. Combination of education with industrial production. etc."[7]

This programme was finalised in January 1848 by Marx and Engels. They, however had given assurances to the people in general and thereby tried to remove all the doubts and suspicions.

Karl Marx and Engels contemplated to consolidate the revolutionary measures in two phases. In the first phase, they would inaugurate a democratic constitution and in the second and final phase, they would abolish private property. They would bring limitation on private property by means of progressive taxation, abolition of inheritance; expropriation of landed proprietors, factory-owners, employment of proletarians in the factories and national estates and paying increased wages, construction of common dwellings, demolition of insanitary dewellings and by abolition of all means of transport.

In his scheme of scientific socialism, there is of course no scope for the state. Bourgeoisie State is "to uphold the system of oppression of one class by another."[8] The state is always "on the side of the rulers." "The class that rules economically that owns the means of production also rules politically."[9] Therefore, the state would be abolished in the Socialist Society.

In the Socialistic Society there would be centralised planning. After socialist revolution became successful, the Union of Soviet Socialist Republic started its first-five-year plan and started planned development. In the first stage of socialism, the principle they follow is, "from each according his ability, to each according to his deeds." At the higher stage of socialist economy, there would be Communist economy, in which the principle would be, "from each according to his ability, to each according to his needs."[10] Due to use of machines and scientific management there would be more production.

In the words of D.D. Kosambi, "socialism is the system where means of production are owned by society as a whole, not private persons, and where opportunity and the rewards of labour are equitably proportionated under the slogan 'equal pay for equal work.' Communism is a more developed form under which individual contributes to society according to his ability and receives a share of the social product according to his needs. Both of them imply a high degree of modern, mechanised, co-operative production before there can be more than a redistribution of poverty."[10(a)]

However, they assured that, the Communists are not interested in the abolition of property in general, but they are interested in abolition of bourgeoisie property; or the private property. They would not abolish the self-acquired, self-earned property; property of the Petty-artisan and the property of small peasant.

The present damage to culture, morality and family would be prevented by abolishing the private property. They want to rescue education from the influence of the ruling class. The communists will do away with the present status of women as mere instruments of production.

The Communists are further reproached with desiring to abolish countries and nationality.[11] They Think think that 'the working men have no country.' They think that exploitation of an individual by another is put to end, the exploitation of one nation by another will also be put to an end.

The protagonist of freedom of thought and expression would criticise on the Communists as they prevent any thought going against them. However, Marx says that, "the ruling ideas of each age have ever been the ideas of its ruling class."[12] The fact is the Communist will rupture the Traditional Ideas only and not modern and progressive ideas.

However, Paul M. Sweezy states that "neither Marx nor (so far as I know) any other modern socialist of importance-ever advocated or expected that private ownership of consumer goods would or should be abolished. On the contrary, he favoured the multiplication of consumer goods in the hands of the lower-income groups, hence a great extension of private ownership in this sphere.

As to the form of ownership of the means of production which would characterise, Socialism, Marxists have never been dogmatic. Ownership must be by public bodies, but that does not necessarily mean only the central government : local governments, special public authorities of one sort or another, and co-operatives can also own means of production under socialism. And there can even be a certain amount of private ownership, provided it is confined to industries in which production takes place on a small scale."[13]

While pointing out the weakness of Marxist Philosophy, Jaiprakash Narayan has said that, "If you go back to the classics of socialism, you will not get much light, because neither Marx nor Engels, nor Kauntsky nor Lenin described in detail the Political Characteristics of a Socialist Society. Marx and Engels, as you know, were mostly concerned with analysing the capitalist society and finding out the dynamic of that society which would help the socialists to create out of capitalism a socialist society."[13(a)]

Karl Marx advocated for imposing dictatorship of Proletariat during the days of Transition from capitalism to socialism. In the days of Marx sufferage was limited, and feudal lords and the priestly class had great influence on the opinion of the Praletarian. They being ignorant and poor were prone to succumb the influence of the capitalist. Consequently, Marx had no faith in democratic institutions at all. Therefore, he recommonds to have dictatorship of the Proletariat till communistic society is fully established. However, he has not said as to how long that period of transition would last.

According to Marx, religion is the opium of the people. The priestly class is always in league with the capitalist class. Therefore, there would be total ban an all religion all morality so that they would not continue their traditional orthodox activities. However, Lenin seems to have softened the views of Marx on religion. Lenin "included the demands for unrestricted freedom of conscience and for separation of church from state and of school from Church."[14] Acoording to Lenin, "Everybody must be perfectly free, not only to profess whatever religion he pleases—but also to change his religion. There should be no established religion or church. All religions and all churches should have equal status in the state."[15] This implies that Lenin had to adhere to public opinion, though conflicting with the views of Marx.

[B] State-socialism

Dr. Babasaheb Ambedkar had developed among others the theory of State-scoialism in his book 'State and Minorities', originally prepared to submit to the Constituent Assembly in March 1947 for the purpose of its consideration, on behalf of The Scheduled Castes Federation.

Accordingly, State socialism envisages, "to put an obligation on the state to plan the economic life of the people on lines which would lead to the highest point of productivity without closing every avenue to private enterprise, and also provide for the equitable distribution of wealth."[16]

He thought that the state should be under obligation to plan the economic life of the people. The social order which he visualises is based on the basic postulates of 'liberty, equality and fraternity'. In his social order, everybody is at liberty to acquire property, tools and materials as being necessary for earning a living to keep the body in due state of health. He states that men are different from each other in respect of heredity, social atmosphere and his own deeds, but they should be given equal opportunity for their development.

He said that, "the connection between individual liberty and the shape and form of an economic structure of society may not be apparent to everyone. Nonethless the connection between the two is real."[17] Undoubtedly, "The individual is an end in himself."[18] Every individual has certain inalienable rights which must be guaranteed to him by the Constitution. However, in the economic system based on private enterprise the rights of individuals are undermined, if not violated. He states that unemployement and fear of starvation may compell him to lose his rights provided under the Constitution.

Therefore, he was of the opinion that it is not enough to enunciate fundamental rights in the Constitution, but to create suitable economic situation in which everybody would be able to enjoy the rights. He does not agree with the proposition that where the state refrains from intervention what remains is liberty. When the state refrains from intervening in the economic life of the people, there would be liberty, but that liberty would be to the capitalists to enslave the poor and nothing more. He therefore, states that the state should fulfil its obligation towards the society in maintaining triple object of liberty, equality and fraternity.

He states that, the state should formulate such a plan

which would lead "to highest point of productivity."[19] It is true that unless the nation increases its production, it can not meet the needs of people. If there is no sufficient production, there can not be adequate and equitable distribution. Moreover, it is necessary to reduce the pressure of population on production, as such people should resort to family planning. The state should make available the avenues of employment and self-employment. The waters flowing from the rivers should be properly utilised by connecting river water by canals. He said that big projects like Damodar Valley projects should be constructed for multiple purposes, like irrigation, transport, flood controls, production of electricity etc. He was in favour of industrialisation and urbanisation and all modern amentities.

In order to avoid concentration of means of production and to avoid exploitation of one class by another, there should be equitable distribution of national wealth. Therefore, he proposes as under:

1. The key industries or which may be declared to be key industries shall be owned and run by the state.
2. The industries which are not key industries but which are basic industries shall be owned by the state and shall be run by the state, or by the corporations established by the state.
3. The insurance shall be a monopoly of the state.
4. Agriculture shall be state industry.

   It shall be organised on the following basis:

   (i) The state shall divide the land into farm of standard size, and let out the farms for cultivation to residents of the village as tenants, made up of group of families to cultivate the land collectively and inaccordance with rules and direction issued by the Government.

   (ii) The tenants shall share among themselves in the manner prescribed, the produce of the farm left after the payment of charges properly leviable on the farm.

(iii) The land shall be let out to villagers without distinction of caste or creed and in such manner that, "there shall be no landlord, no tenant and no landless labourers."

(iv) It shall be obligatory on the part of the state to finance the cultivation of the collective farms by the supply of water, draft animals, implements, manures etc.

(v) The state shall be entitled to levy the following charges on the produce of the farm.

(a) a portion for land revenue;

(b) a portion to pay the debenture holders, and;

(c) a portion to pay for the use of capital goods supplied;

(vi) The state shall prescribe penalty against those tenants who wilfully break the condition or neglect to make best use of the means of cultivation or otherwise act prejudicially to the scheme of collective farm.

(vii) The state shall finance for industry and see that there will be rapid industrialisation and maximum production.

7. In this state socialism avenues of private enterprises are open to all the promising entrepreneurs. He proposes nationalisation of key and basic industries including land, but leaves other industries for the private enterprise. It implies that there is ban on private property in his state socialism. Private property may exist in the form of small scale and cottage industries, personal savings, domestic animals, and other means of production for his maintenance. In his scheme, no person shall be disqualified to hold any public office or exercise any trade or calling by reason of his or her religion, caste, sex or social status. There would be sufficient scope to the enterprising, intelligent and industrious person to undertake any private business.

He had been proposing and professing the philosophy of socialism, including nationalisation of key and basic industries since a very long. The programme of the Independent Labour Party, founded by him in 1936 incorporated. "The principle of state management and state ownership of industry wherever it may become necessary in the interest of the people."[20] The Scheduled Castes Federation, the next party founded by him in 1942 also specifically states in its election manifesto declared in 1951, that, "where national undertaking of an industry is possible and essential, the Scheduled Castes Federation will support national undertaking."[21]

Even in his speech made in Rajya Sabha on 19th March, 1955, he said very categorically that, "peasant proprietorship in this process is going to bring about complete ruination of the country. What we want is although I am not a Communist the Russian System of collective farming. That is the only way by which we can solve our agricultural problem."[21(a)]

Then whole scheme of State-socialism would be an intrinsic and inseparable part of the Constitution. There could be three reasons for this provision: (1) There should be continuity in the scheme for the success of planned economy, especially for the long-term plans. If they are discontinued abruptly on any unreasonable ground, it may be futile; (2) It can not be expected; under parliamentary system that the plan would be continued by the new government. One party may agree to it, but it is not certain that the other party would agree to continue it, and (3) In our country, he states that, "the majority is a communal majority." It may try to protect caste interests rather than national interest. Probably they may not tolerate the poor and weaker sections taking benefit of planned development.

Then whether to accept dictatorial form of Government in place of parliamentary democracy in order to secure permanence for the successful working of the economic plans? He did not like to exchange parliamentary democracy for dictatorship for the continuity of state socialism. He states that, "the way out seems to be to retain parliamentary democracy and to prescribe state socialism by the law of the Constitution so that it will be beyond the reach of a parliamentary majority to suspend, amend or abrogate it. It is only by this that one can achieve the Triple object, namely, to establish socialism, retain parliamentary democracy and avoid dictatorship."[22]

Generally, the Constitutions provide for political structure of the nation, leaving the economic structure to be decided by the ensuing Parliament and the ruling party. Therefore, he emphatically said , "time has come to take a bold step and define both the economic structure as well as the political structure of society by the law of the Constitution."[23] If the Constitution is confined to mere adult sufferage and fundamental rights and governmental machinery it would be of no avail. It may promote the value of "one man one vote", but not "one man one value."

It is a fact that the proposed scheme of 'state-socialism' could not be included in the Constitution verbatim, but it can not be said that, "he could not make our Constitution really socialistic, he was required to give up his idea of the inclusion of his socialist thoughs in the Indian Constitution."[23(a)] It is however a fact that the Constitution of India had incorporated "Directive Principles of State Policy", and thereby the principles of socialism. While responding to a question raised as to the nature of the Directive Principles, Dr. Babasaheb Ambedkar said stell that, "If these directive principles to which I have drawn attention are not socialistic in their direction and in their content, I fail to understand what more socialism can be."[24] Thus, he provided the object sprit and content of socialism in the form of directive principles of the State Policy in part IV of the Constitution of India. Although they are not enforceable by any court, they are "fundamental in the governance of the country, and it shall be the duty of the state to apply these principles in making laws."[25] It has been specifically laid down, among others, that, "the state shall strive to promote the welfare of the people by securing and protecting as effectively as it may a social order in which justice, social, economic and political shall iniform all the institutions of the national life"[26] that, "The State shall in particular, direct its policy towards securing" "that the citizens, men and women equally, have the right to an adequate means of livelihood."[27] "that the ownership and control of the material resources of the community are so distributed as best to subserve the common good.[28] That the operation of the economic system does not result in the concentration of wealth and means of production to the common detriment."[29] Howfar these Constitutional Directives, and the laws and rules based on these directives are being implemented in their proper perspective is a different question and beyond the scope of the present study.

Dr. Babasaheb Ambedkar had an unflinching and indomitable faith in democracy. He had no approabation for dictatorship at all. Referring to Russian dictatorship in those days, he states that "Humanity does not only want economic values; it also wants spiritual values to be retained. Permanent dictatorship has paid no attention to spiritual values and does not seem to intend to. Carlyle called political economy a pig philosophy. Carlyle was of course wrong, for man needs material comforts. Man must grow materially as well as spiritually. Society has been aiming to lay a new foundation was summarised by the French Revolution in three words, fraternity, liberty and equality. The French Revolution was welcomed because of this slogan. It failed to produce equality. We welcome the Russian Revolution because it aims to produce equality. But it cannot be too much emphasised that in producing equality society can not afford to sacrifice fraternity or liberty. Equality will be of no value without fraternity or liberty. It seems that the three can co-exist only if one follows the way of the Buddha. Communism can give one but not all."[30]

He said Buddha realised that "what is necessary is not escape from the world. What is necessary is to change the world and to make it better."[31] He has rightly said that, "my ideal would be a society-based on liberty, equality and fraternity."[32] Thus, he contemplated to reconstruct the society on the long cherished values of liberty, equality and fraternity.

Conclusion

Thus, both, Karl Marx and Babasaheb Ambedkar advocated for rooting out capitalism, feudalism and socio-economic exploitation from the society and reconstruct the society on the basis of modern values of liberty, equality and fraternity.

Marx totally opposed to Bourgeoisie hegemony whereas Babasaheb Ambedkar squarely opposed to Brahmanic hegemony, caste system, untouchability and servitude.

Both of them thought to abolish private property being root cause of poverty, exploitation and class-war. Karl Marx wanted to establish scientific socialism whereas Babasaheb thought, to bring into reality his State-socialism.

Karl Marx thought that after attaining scientific socialism the state will wither away. Babasaheb Ambedkar thought that the state would be under obligation to bring into reality the ideal society. For both of them socialism is not only a economic system, but an ideal social, cultural and political system.

Notes and References

1. Watkins Frederick: *The Age of Ideology,* p. 47. Prentice-Hall of India Pvt. Ltd. New Delhi. (1965).
2. DBAWS: Vol. III, p. 443.

3. *Ibid.*,Vol.I. p. 411.
4. *Ibid*,. p. 409.
5. Encyclopadeia Britanica, Vol. 10, p. 926.
6. Marks-Engels: *The Socialist Revolution*, p. 50-51.
7. Karl Marx and F. Engels: Manifesto of the Communist Party, pp. 75-76.
   Peoples Publishing House (P) Ltd. New Delhi (2012).
8. Huberman and Sweezy: *Introduction to Socialism*, p. 34.
9. *Ibid.*, p. 35.
10. *Ibid.*, p. 67.

10(a) Kosambi D.D. Exhasparated Essays, p. 35.

11. Marx-Engels: *The Socialist Revolution*, p. 73.
12. *Ibid.*, p. 74.
13. Huberman-Sweezy: *Introduction to Socialism,* pp. 83-84.

13(a) Prasad Bimla (Ed.) Socialism Sarvodaya and Democracy, p.104. Asia Publishing House, Bombay-1. (1964).

14. Barmenkov A. Freedom of Conscience in the USSR. p. 18.
15. Ibid., p. 19.
16. DBAWS: Vol. I: p. 408.
17. *Ibid.*, p. 409.
18. *Ibid.*, p. 409.
19. *Ibid.*, p. 408.
20. Khairmode C.B. Dr. Bhimrao R. Ambedkar: Charitra Ganth, Vol. 6 and 7. p. 11.
    Maharashtra Rajya Sahitye Sanskrit Mandal, Mumbai., (1985)
21. *Ibid.*, Vol. 10, p. 153.

21(a) Khairmode Vol. II, p. 161.

22. *Ibid.*, Vol. I, p. 412.
23. DBAWS. p. 412.

23(a) An article by B.R.Joshi, The Philosophy of Dr. B.R. Ambedkar as reflected in the Indian Constitution, the Philosophy of Dr. B.R. Ambedkar, Edited by Pradeep Gokhale, Sugava Pune (2008) pp. 172-173.

24. DBAWS. Vol. 13, p. 326.
25. The Constitution of India, 1950, Art. 37
26. *Ibid.*, Article 38 (1)
27. *Ibid.*, Article 39 (a)
28. *Ibid.*, Article 39 (b)
29. *Ibid.*, Article 39 (c)
30. DBAWS: Vol. 3. p. 462.
31. *Ibid.*, Vol. II, p. 112.
32. *Ibid.*, Vol. I, p. 57.

8

Vision and Mission

[A]

In Germany and neighbouring states Karl Marx witnessed that a grim situation of strife between Proletariat and Bourgeoisie Classes was rampant. The main cause of struggle was persistently prevailing strained relations between those two classes because of exploitation of Proletariat by the Bourgeoisie Class. Economically, the Proletariat were poor and day by day they were in wretched condition; whereas the Bourgeoisie were rich and day by day they were becoming rich and were in dominating position. Due to their rich position they were dominating all the aspects of social life and holding their exploitative control over the political power. The feudals and clergymen were in league with them. Ultimately, the Proletariat were deprived of all the fruits of industrialization and affluence.

Compassionate Marx thought seriously as to how the Proletariat could be emancipated from growing wretchedness and serfdom. He eventually came to the conclusion that, "their ends can be attained only by the forcible overthrow of all existing social conditions. Let the ruling classes tremble at a communistic revolution. The Proletarians have nothing to lose but their chains. They have a World to Win." Therefore, the *Manifesto of the Communist Party* gave a clarion call to "working men of all countries, unite !"[1]

Thus, the vision of Karl Mavx was clear and crystal. He was determined to emancipate the Proletariat Class and establish a new social order, based on scientific socialism or communism.

Dr. Babasaheb Ambedkar, as a social scientist has rightly comprehended and epitomised the principles propounded by Karl Marx, and called it as, "The original creed of Karl Marx". Accordingly, the basic principles of the creed of Karl Marx are as under:

(i) "That the purpose of philosophy is to reconstruct the world and not to explain the origin of the universe.

(ii) That the forces which shape the course of history are primarily economic.

(iii) That the society is divided into two classes, owners and workers.

(iv) That there is always a class conflict going on between the two classes.

(v) That the workers are exploited by the owners, who misappropriate the surplus value which is the result of the workers labour.

(vi) That this exploitation can be put an end to by nationalisation of the instruments of production, i.e., abolition of private property.

(vii) That this exploitation is leading to greater and greater impoverishment of the workers.

(viii) That this growing impoverishment of the workers is resulting in a revolutionary spirit among the workers and the conversion of the class conflict into a class-struggle.

(ix) That as the workers outnumber the owners, the workers are bound to capture the state and establish their rule which he called the dictatorship of the proletariat.

(x) These factors are irresistable and therefore socialism is inevitable.[2]

Karl Marx was a compassionate thinker. He has taken active interest in the liberation of the toiling masses in the world. He endeavoured to bring a new light to them directly or through his companions, tried to organise them and inspired to struggle against all the exploitative forces. His contribution to the toiling masses and the world Communist movement could be summarised as under:

1. On European Affairs

(a) *Problem of Belgium*:

Belgium came under the rule of Austria from 1713. Later on, France took over Belgium. After the expulsion of Napoleon, the Congress of Vienna (1814-15) gave Belgium to the Netherlands. However, in 1830 the Belgians rebelled against Dutch rule and declared their independence.

"Under the monarchical rule of King Leopold, his soldiers were asked to disperse foreign fugitives in Belgium and prohibit any democratic propaganda and public meetings. Even the Police arrested Karl Marx for anti-Bourgyeoisie propaganda. When his wife, Jenny Marx went to inquire about the whereabouts of Marx, to the Police Station, the Police, arrested her and "held for one night in the company of common prostitutes."[3] However, the order of arrest was taken back. Later on Marx decided to leave Brussels for Paris; in February 1848.

(b) *Polish Insurrection of 1863-64*:

Poland was previously belonged to Tsarist Russia. The national liberation insurrection broke out in the Polish lands in January 1863. Marx and Engels, however thought that, if support is given to the Polish, it could spark revolution in Europe. Marx and Engels kept a watch over the struggle and kept corresponding to each other. The big land owners were finding ways and means to put down the peasants revolution in Russia and Poland. France and England were also not in favour of Polish insurrection. "On February 8, 1863, the Tsarist and Prussian governments signed a convention on joint suppression of the insurgents."[4] Karl Marx did his utmost in support of the Polish Insurgents. He asked the German workers to support the poles and started a fund raising campaign among the German workers in England, Switzerland, the United States and Germany.

(*c*) *Coup in Prussia*:

It was on November 2, 1848 King Friedrich Wilhelm IV asked the reactionary forces to form a new Government in Prussia. Therefore, Marx asked the people of Prussia to refuse to pay taxes and to unite the country's progressive forces, so as to frustrate the plans of the counter-revolutionary forces. Marx signed an appeal which contained three slogans:

(1) resistance to the forcible collection of taxes by every possible means.

(2) organisation of people's volunteer detachments to beat back the enemy; and

(3) establishment of safety committees to confront authorities refusing to abide by the National Assembly's decision. Hence, Marx was arrested. The supporters of Marx gathered outside the court and gave slogans to free Marx. He was, however freed. Due to mounting force, the King dissolved the National Assembly and promised to convene new chambers very soon and announced the granting of a Prussion Constitution.[5]

In 1862 Bismark became the Prime-Minister of Prussia. France under the rule of Louis Napolean (Second Empire) attacked on Prussia in 1870. In the Franco - Prussion War (1870-71) France was defeated. It created a United Germany. Ultimately, the German Empire was founded (with Prussia) on 18th January 1871; and King Wilhelm 1 of Prussia was proclaimed Emperor of Germany at Verscilles; and Bismark became the Chancellor.

Marx thought the socio-economic conditions were very ripe for Proletarian revolution in Germany. August Bebel founded the German Socialist-Democratic Workers' party in 1869. He was a staunch Marxist.

(d) *Irish Problem*:

Before formation of free Ireland in 1921, the whole territory was under the British rule since a very long period. Therefore, the movement to free Ireland from British rule was in vogue. In 1867, the pro-independence Fenian people attacked the wagan carrying two Fenian prisoners and freed them, who were arrested on the charges of a coup.[6] In the incident one of the police escort was killed. Therefore, some of the persons from the masses were arrested on a charge of murder, they were brought before the court and the court sentenced them to death. Hence, the prison wall was blown up by the Fenians in which twelve people were killed. Consequently, the British government treated the Fenians as common criminals although they were political rebels.

Karl-Marx and Engels were on the side of independence movement and working class. The Irish workers formed their autonomous rule. However, there arose a rift between the Irish workers and the British workers. Marx devoted all his energies for the emancipation of Ireland. Marx thought that "the freedom of Irish people was a necessary condition for the emancipation of the English working class, on which, in its turn, the emancipation of the European Proletariat depended."[7] Hence, he thought to overthrow the English landed Oligarchy from Ireland.

The English Bourgeoisie and the English aristocracy had a common interest in turning Ireland into a mere "pasture-land" to provide the English market with meat and wool at the lowest possible prices. Moreover, owing to the increasing concentration of tenant farming Ireland provided a steady surplus of its population for the English labour market, causing depressing wages and the material and moral position of the English working class. "In all the industrial and commercial centres of England the working class was divided into two hostile camps: the English workers on the one hand and their Irish fellow wokers on the other. The ordinary English worker hated the Irish worker as a competitor, and felt himself superior as a member of the dominant race."[8] The International Workingmen's Association also was not able to solve this problem. Marx urged the General Council to support the Irish movement, which demanded an amnesty for the irregularly condemned Fenians. The British Government was not ready to grant amnesty to the Irish People.

(e) *Social Change in Russia:*

Marx kept a close watch on internal developments in Russia. Its defeat in Crimean War in 1850 exposed its weaknesses.

Lopatin Danielson wrote Marx concerning publication of Capital in Russian. He went to London in 1870, and met Marx. On Marx's advice Lopatin began translation of the book. However, after coming to Russia, he was arrested and he was not free till 1873. The Russian translation came out on March 27, 1872. By the end of the year almost all 3000 copies were sold. (Vol. I).

It helped Russian to spread Marxism in Russia. The Russian edition of *Manifesto of the Communist Party* came out in 1882. During his work in the International, Marx continued to keep a close watch on the foreign policy of Tsarist Russia.[9] He was in the knowledge of all happenings in Russia virtually from 1850 onwards. The Russian Section of the International was setup in Geneva in 1870.

Lenin's "study of Marx had convinced him that sometime the nationalistic system was bound to crack up." He believed that "the time for the crush of nationalism had come, and he looked for something to replace it."[10]

Landed estates and resultant dependence of the

Peasants on their old masters, were the impediments in the way of progressive economic development.

Marx and his companions were mainly responsible in consolidating Marxism in Russia. Therefore Communist revolution became successful in 1917.

(*f*) *Unification of Italy*:

In early 1859 Italy was on the verge of a revolutionary outbreak. It was necessary to liberate its northern part (Lombardy and Venice) from Austrian rule. The unification - under the leadership of Count Cavour, a rich landowner was complete. However, there were successful uprisings in Tuscany, Parma and Modena. The absolutist regimes in these states were overthrown. Uprisings also occurred in Romagna and other Papal Provinces.[11]

Marx supported the Patriotic forces. He praised the exposure by Mazzini; the leader of the Italian democrats, of Napalean III's counter-revoluting plans with respect to Italy.[12]

The war, however ended with the Treaty on July 11, 1859. Revolutionaries could not defeat the forces of reactionary. Lombardy was handed over to France and later to the Savoy dynasty.

Subsequently, the Revolutionists under the leadership of Garibaldi gave fight in April 1860 for unification of Italy.

At the end of October 1860, a Plebiscite in Southern Italy supported her integration with the Kingdom of Piedmont of the Savoy dynasty.[13] The Socialist party of Italy was founded in 1892 to propagate the programme of socialism.

2. On Civil-War in U.S.A.

In the United States of America the Negroes were subjected to racial discrimination, segregation and involuntary servitude by the white people. It was rampant conspicuously in the eleven southern states of the USA. However, there was no cohesion among the people and the movement of the Blacks or Negroes. Therefore, there was conflict between Blacks versus Whites, Southern States versus Northern States and Liberals versus Conservatives.

However, in the Presidential election held in March, 1861, the liberal Republican Party candidate Abraham Lincoln was elected President. This was an obvious jolt to the Pro-slavery White people of the Southern States. Hence, the disappointed and enraged eleven southern states which wanted to retain slavery of the Blacks, reacted by breaking away from the Union and forming the Confederate states of America. Eventually, it gave rise to civil-war in the USA Eventually, President Abraham Lincoln signed the proclamation of Emancipation on 22nd September 1862 'as a war measure.'

In consonance with the Proclamation the Congress passed the Thirteenth, Fourteenth and Fifteenth Amendments to the US Constitution.

The Thirteenth Amendment (1865) provided that, "Neither slavery nor involuntary servitude...... shall exist within the United States, or any place subject to its jurisdiction."

The Fourteenth Amendment (1868) provided that, "All persons born or naturalised in the United States, and subject to the jurisdiction thereof, are citizens of the United States and of the State wherein they reside."

The Fifteenth Amendment (1870) provided that, "The right of citizens of the United States to vote shall not be denied or abridged by the United States or by any state on account of race, colour or previous condition of servitude."[14]

In order to subdue the rebellious secessionist southern states President Abraham Lincoln had to wage a war against them. Ultimately, they surrendered on 9th April 1865, making the end of the American Civil War. President Lincoln had successfully proved to be the champion of equality, but he was assassinated in 1865 itself.

It is now pertinent to see as to what role Karl Marx and his companion played in the problem of emancipation of the Negroes in the USA Karl-Marx being a liberator of the exploited masses and propounder of the egalitarian philosophy had played a very crucial role in the struggle for abolition of slavery in the USA.

Karl Marx was in touch with the US workers through Joseph Weydemeyer and Adolf Cluss, both members of the Communist League. Marx's friends endeavoured to spread communism in USA through a newspaper 'Die Reform' started in March 1853. It became the organ of the Labour Union; but it was closed in 1854.

During the civil-war which broke in 1861 in USA Marx naturally stood for abolition of slavery of the Negroes. He thought that, "the abolition of slavery in the USA by revolutionary means would give a powerful impetus to the liberation struggle on either side of the Atlantic. That is why he attached such importance to solidarity between the European working class and the American Abolitionists, and the oppressed Negroes themselves."[14(a)]

Marx wrote over 40 articles[14(b)] on the civil-war in *Tribune* in favour of abolition of the slavery in Southern Part of America. It served the purpose to a great extent. However, due to influence of the pro-slavery bourgeoisie the Tribune declined further to publish his articles.

However, the workers in London, Manchester and Sheffield organised meetings in support of the fighters against Negro Slavery in 1862, and 1863, and shown their sympathy and solidarity with them. Karl Marx himself was present in the workers meeting held at St. James Hall, London, on 26th March 1863, organised by the London Trades Council in support of the Blacks. Eventually, the Confederate forces surrendered in April 1865.

3. On British Colonialism in India

The British East-India Company established its Power in India in eighteenth century itself. It was fully consolidated with the fall of Peshwa rule in 1818, and with the defeat of remaining rulers in 1857. Their policy of new land tenure system, however gave rise to Landlordism as a result of which the petty teanats, agricultural labourers and small shopkeepers were living in poor wretched condition. The depressed classes were the worst sufferers of the system. Their position was very much deplorable as compared to the Negroes in America and the proletariats in Europe. They were, however, subjected to untouchability, involuntary servitude and inhuman treatment. They were politically subjugated, socially depressed, economically exploited, educationally deprived and culturally oppressed. They were everywhere treated as *persona-non-grata*. Although the Britishers tried to bring about some change in the society introducing some politico-legal reforms, there was no change in the life of the Depressed Classes. Karl-Marx, though distantly aware of the unjust Indian Social System, who had shown his full sympathy to the Negroes and exploited people in the world, had failed to take due cognizance of the worst suffering masses of India, the Depressed Classes. He, however wrote articles, "The British rule in India", "The East India Company its history and results", and "the future results of the British rule in India."[15]

Marx, however takes due notice of the village system prevailing in those days in India from the fifth report of the select committee on the affairs of the East India Company (London 1812) as under—

"Every village is, and appears always to have been, in fact a separate community or republic. Officials :

(1) The Potail, Goud, Mundil *etc.,* as he is termed in different languages, is the head inhabitant, who has generally the superitendence of the affairs of the village, settles the disputes of the inhabitants, attends to the police and performs the duty of collecting the revenue within the village...

(2) The Curnam, Shanbog, or Putwaree, is the register.

(3) The Taliary or Sthulwar and

(4) The Totie, are severally the Watchmen of the village and the Crops.

(5) The Neerguntee distributes the water of the streams or reservoirs in just proportion to the several fields.

(6) The Joshee or astrologer, announces the seed-times and harvests, and lucky or unlucky days or hours for all the operation of farming.

(7) The Smith, and

(8) The Carpenter frame the rude instruments of husbandry, and the ruder dwellings of the farmer.

(9) The Potter fabricates the only utensils of the village.

(10) The waterman keeps clean the few garments.

(11) The barber,

(12) The Silver Smith, who often combines the function of village poet and schoolmaster. Then the Brahmin, for worship."[15(a)]

He perceived the Indian Society as in, "Unchanging and Unresisting State", but he could not fully expose the prevailing exploitative system to a great extent; with special reference to the so-called untouchables; nor he could proclaim his solidarity with them. Probably, he could not perceive the seriousness of the problem due to lack of knowledge and information to that effect.

4. On Experiment of Commune

It was on the advice and approval of Karl Marx and Engels the proletariats in Paris established "Communes".

In the preface to the new German edition of the *Communist Manifesto,* dated 24th June 1872, Karl Marx and Engels state that, "in view of the practical experience gained, first in the February Revolution, and then, still more, in the Paris Commune, where the proletariat for the first time held political power for two whole months, this programme has in some details become antiquated. One thing especially was proved by the Commune, *viz.*, that, "the working class can not simply" lay hold of the readymade state machinery, and wield it for its own purposes."[16]

The Commune means, in the words of Karl Marx (The civil war in France), "The direct anti-thesis to the empire." It was the "specific form" of "a republic that was not only to remove the monarchical form of class rule, but rule itself...."[17]

The Programme and organisation of the Communes were based on the following principles:

1. The first decree of the Commune was the suppression of the standing army, and its replacement by the armed people.
2. The Commune was formed of the municipal councillors, chosen by Universal suffrage in the various wards of Paris.
3. The majority of them were workingmen or their representatives.
4. The police were stripped of its political attributes and became responsible instrument of the commune.
5. Other officers also were made responsible instrument of the Commune.
6. The privileges of all the officers were withdrawn.
7. The powers of the priests were withdrawn.
8. The judicial functionaries lost their independence. They became elective and responsible.
9. The commune was to be the political form of even the smallest village.... and the Communes were to elect the "National Delegation," in Paris.

It was, however not a federation of scattered units. Marx had no faith in federalism. "Marx was a centralist."[18] However, the small units or communes were not capable in crushing the resistance of the capitalists. They were also not capable in transferring the privately owned land, factories and means of communications *etc.*, to the nation. Ultimately, the communes proved to be unsuccessful. The communes were in existence practically for two months only.

In the words of Thomas Mathew, "Marx could hail the Paris Commune as the model of mankind's emancipation from oppression and tyranny."[18(a)]

5. Organisations Founded

(*a*) *Communist League*: (1846-1848)

In early 1846 Marx and Engels formed the Brussels Communist correspondence committee (1846). The object of the said committee was, obviously to spread communism in various countries. It was decided to carry on correspondence with workers and socialist leaders and organisations in varous countries. The committee established contacts with English chartists, and the league of just in London (1836). The leaders of the just were convinced that Marx and Engels would properly lead the socialist movement. Ultimately, the Congress was held in London in early June 1847. At the Congress the League of just was renamed the Communist League. Marx and Engels, however joined the league. The new rules were drafted. "The Congress decided to drop the old vague motto," "All Men are Brethren !" and to adopt the attractive and meaningful motto "Working men of all Countries, Unite !"[19]

"The establishment of the Communist League, the first international working class organisation which proclaimed scientific communism to be its ideological banner, was an event of great importance in the history of the proletariat's emancipation struggle. It inaugurated the fusion of Marxism and the working-class movement, and heralded the future triumph of the Marxist outlook and the ideas of international proletarian solidarity."[20]

The second Congress was held from November 29 to December, 1847. It was attended by delegates from Germany, France, England, Switzerland and Belgium. Marx and Engels were present in the meeting. They were assigned the responsibility of drafting the principles and programmes of the Communist Party. The drafting of the *'Communist Manifesto'* was completed in January 1848. The manuscript of the manifesto was firstly in Germany. It was published in Frech in Paris. It exerted a great effect on the working people in France. However, the Democratic Revolution successfully took place in France in February 1848 under Louis Napolean (Nephew of Napolean). The Proletarian Revolutionists thinking to take the benefit of the situation of transition and turmoil rose against the bourgeoise—democratic government in June 23 to 26, 1848. However, the revolutionary forces were desperately defeated.[21]

In the meantime. The Prussian government in a bid to suppress the Proletarit sent its force on the Central Board of the Communist League located in Cologne. The members were arrested and tried in October 1852. On 12th November 1852, seven of the Proletariats were found guilty of treason and sentenced from three to six years. Subsequently, the Communist League was dissolved.

"The Communist League was much too weak to act alone in the work of accelerating the revolutionary movement, and it was soon seen that its reorganisation on the continent was only in its infancy. However, this was no longer so important because the working class had now won the means, and the possibility of conducting its propoganda openly, and therefore, the primary reason for the existence of the Communist League was removed."[22]

However, with the initiative of Karl Marx and Engels the Communist League was revived in March 1850. On 15th September 1850 the Central Committee of League was convened, but there arose a rift in the league. Ultimately, the league came to end.

Later, in May 1851 the members of the Communist League were arrested while propagating Communist literature. The Prussion Police booked a case of treason against eleven members of the League. However, seven out of eleven were found guilty, as such they were sentenced to different punishments at Cologne.[23] Karl Marx, Engels and other important Members of the League were very much busy in the trial and had to be very careful for their next movement.

(b) *International Working men's Associations*

It was necessary to establish an international organisation of the Communists all over the world. It was necessited because the capitalist mode of production was an embodiment of contradicton. So long as the capitalist mode of production exists the contradictions exist. Hence, there can not be brotherhood of men at national and international levels. Although the large scale industrialists preached freedom and peace between nations for the development of international Trade and Commerce, bifurcated the world into an armed camp and intensified the fierce competition.

The declaration of *"The Communist Manifesto"* that United action on the part of the Proletariat in all 'civilised countries' was necessary, naturally made a tremendous impact on the Proletariat class. It was because of this favourable atmosphere Napolean Bonapart repealed the penal provisions in 1864 which provided punishment for workers convicted of joining combinations or unions.[24] Even some of the new unions turned their attention to the question of reforming the franchise.

Thus, having taken into account the importance of united action of the Proletariat and its benefits, Karl Marx and Engels thought to establish an organisation of the international stature to lead the workingmen in the world. Thus, the first international mass organisation of the Proletariat, named the International Workingmen's Association, was established amidst the delegates from England and France and the members of various organisations at a meeting held in St. Martin's Hall, London, on 28th September 1864. It was presided over by Professor

Beesly. Karl Marx himself drafted the provisional rules of the Association and presented its inaugural address to the delegates.

The preamble of the Rules of the International provided, among others, that, "the emancipation of the working classes must be conquered by the working classes themselves, the goal of the Proletariat was to abolish all class-rule."[25]

The meeting of the General Council was held on April 25, 1865, and secondly at Geneva in 1866. Thirdly, it met at Brussels (1968), and Later at Basle (1869). The Basle Congress championed the socialisation of land and collective ownership of the means of production. The next Congress was held in London in 1871 and at Hague in 1872, Later it met at Amasterdam. However, due to internal dissentions the International Working men's Association was dissolved in 1874. In the words of Yuri Sdobnikov, "Its services to the international working class and Communist movements, and to subsequent generations of staunch fighters against tyranny of capital for social progress and communism, will never be forgotten."[26]

"His life in Politics", said Volkov, was inseparable from his life in science, one sphere of activity fertilised and stimulated the other. And in both occasion, fought equally mercilessly for the purity of ends and means, considerating all deviations from this as shameful."[27]

"It soon became clear," states Franz Mehring, "That Marx was the actual "head" of the movement. Not that he pushed himself forward in anyway for he had an unlimited contempt for all cheap popularity, and unlike those Democrats who made ethemselves look important in Public whilst in reality doing nothing, he did a tremendous amount of work behind of scenes whilst at the same time keeping himself well out of the Public view." "to a far greater extent than in Cologne Marx was now in position to exercise his incomparable gift of mastering men by teaching and leading them."[28]

(B)

Indian Society is a conglomeration of thousands of castes, sub-castes and communities. They are divided religiously, linguistically, culturally and geographically. Apart from that they have no common history and common national sentiments. Every Indian lives with false pride of his caste and prejudices against others. They cannot inter-marry nor they can inter-dine. It is formed with an ascending scale of reverence and a descending scale of contempt. There is no endosmosis in the society. In otherwords, there is no social and economic equality. There is lack of sense of brotherhood and unity and integrity.

Apart from these diversities, the Hindu society has produced, the untouchables, who were subjected to 'untouchability' and the criminal and aboriginal tribes sujected to social and spatial segregation. They were *persona non-grata*, not eligible to hold property nor to take education. They were subjected to all cruelty and inhuman treatment.

Not withstanding a very diversified and gloomy state of affairs, Dr. Babasaheb Ambedkar with all magnanimity, liberal and rational attitude decided to reform the Indian Society; especially the so-called Hindu Society on the basis of liberty, equality and fraternity. Thus, he had developed a very broad vision of integrated society to be formed by peaceful and constitutional means. It was, of course not a very easy task but he was fully determined to overcome all the odds and obstacles in his way and reform the Hindu Society.

His vision of society was, however opposed by the vested interests of Brahmanic and capitalistic forces. The Brahmanic forces were not at all ready to allow the so-called untouchables to touch even the common water tank and share the public places. The priestly class was not ready to allow them to enter the temples and worship the idols therein. The Landlords were bent upon exploiting the so-called untouchables as much as possible. They were not ready to spare even a small piece of land for their livelihood. They used to protect the waste land for grazing the cattles but were unwilling to give it to the poor fellows of the so-called untouchable community. They were being oppressed in the name of exploitative *Watandari* or hereditary servitude. The British Government was quite liberal in attitude, but not very sympathetic to the poor untouchables at the cost of their own colonial interests. Thus, there seemed to be unwritten alliance between all the exploitative forces against the interests of the Depressed Classes. Therefore, they were naturally against the vision and mission of emancipation of the Depressed Classes launched by Dr. Babasaheb Ambedkar. His ceaseless struggle for the emancipation of his brethren itself corroborates the fact that he was determined to emancipate them by peaceful way without resorting to revolutionary means and without causing any injury to the national interests. Herein lies his uniqueness and greatness.

The creed of Dr. Babasaheb Ambedkar could be epitomised as under:

1. What is necessary is not escape from the world. What is necessary is to change the world and to make it better.
2. Man is an end in himself. Every one is entitled to equal human rights and privileges and pursuits of happiness, irrespective of caste, creed, religion, sex, place of birth, language and faith.
3. The forces that shape the course of history are primarily social, but inevitably economic and religious.
4. Society is divided into several classes based on certain socio-economic factors and each one is struggling for its existence. Hence, conflict is inherent.
5. Any problem can be solved by constitutional means and not by resorting to violence or force.
6. Socialism is inevitable to maintain socio-economic equality and moral order based on justice, liberty, equality and fraternity.
7. Every idea or phenomenon is subject to inquiry, examination and confirmation.
8. State is imperative to maintain peace and order, to

undertake welfare activities, to encourage scientific invention and industrial and technological development, to protect from foreign aggression and internal dissensions.

9. Buddhism is in consonance with modern science and reason and humanism.
10. Parliamentary form of government is the best form of government.[29]

1. Socio-religious Movement

In order to reform Indian society on the sublime values of liberty, equality and fraternity, Babasaheb Ambedkar started his mission right from 1919 to its virtual fulfilment till his end. He rose from 'Mook Nayak' to 'Prabuddha Nayak' within such a short span of time. He had to form several organizations and launch movements, undertake literary activities and form strategies for liberation of the so called Depressed Classes including the small farmers and toiling labourers.

(a) The first and foremost task before him was to remove ignorance of the untouchables, enlighten their mind with new ideology of liberation, raise their level of understanding and to imbibe in them an ambition to be a ruling class. He, however said emphatically that the caste system and 'untouchability' were deliberately created by the priestly class and supported by the Brahmanic forces including the land lords and caste ridden elements in the society for the protection of their common interests.

In order to evoke a sense of brotherhood and self-respect among the so-called untouchables a conference was convened at Mangaon in the erstwhile Kolhapur State on 21st and 22nd March 1920. It was presided over by Dr. Babasaheb Ambedkar and addressed, among others by the Maharaja of Kolhapur. It was followed by an inter-caste dinner attended by His Highness the Maharaja of Kolhapur, the State

Officials and Dr. Babasaheb Ambedkar and his followers. In the conference, the Maharaja declared that the Depressed Classes got their own true leader and all of them follow him.[30]

(b) In order to invigorate the social consciousness among the untouchable brethren, Dr. Babasaheb Ambedkar established *'Bahishkrit Hitkarini Sabha'* on 20th July 1924 at Bombay. It was aimed.

(i) to promote the spread of education by opening Hostels.

(ii) to promote the spread of culture by opening libraries and social centres.

(iii) to improve economic condition of the 'Depressed Classes' by starting industrial and agricultural schools; and

(iv) to represent the grievances of the 'Depressed Classes.

Its president was Sir Chimanlal Setalvad and Chairman of the managing committee was Dr. Babasaheb Ambedkar, its Secretary was S.N. Shivtarkar and its Treasurer was N.T. Jadhav. There were other respectable persons on its management committee. The Sabha tried to bring about social awareness amongst the untouchables. The main objective of the Sabha was, "educate, agitate and organise."[31]

"In order to awaken the untouchables, he gave the slogan, "Tell the slave he is slave, he will revolt."[32] The slogan proved to be true. He has categorically said that the untouchables would not get anything by begging. They have to manifest their strength and vigour."[33]

(*c*) In view of the S.K. Bole Resolution passed by the Legislative Council of the Bombay Presidency, which removed the disabilities of the untouchables and allowed to use Public Watering Places, Wells and Dharmashalas maintained by the government, the Depressed Classes people decided to claim their right to equality and launch the famous *Choudar Tank Satyagraha* at Mahad on 19th and 20th March 1927; under the Leadership of Dr. Babasaheb Ambedkar and his followers. The *Satyagraha* was launched peacefully, but on some false provocation, the Caste Hindus violently attacked on the *Satyagra* his. Later on, it was reorganised on 25th December 1927, and burnt Manusmriti and proclaimed their symbolic protest against the unjust Hindu Dharmashastras.

(*d*) Further, Ambedkar launched the famous temple entry *Satyagraha* at Kalaram Temple at Nasik alongwith his followers on 2nd March 1930. It was, however in continuation intermittantly for five years, but in vain. When the Hindu Orthodox mind was not willing to allow equal religious rights to the Depressed classes, Dr. Babasaheb Ambedkar declared to renounce Hindu religion, at Yeola (Nasik) on 13th October 1935. In the meantime, Temple entry *Satyagra* has were launched at several places including the Ambadevi Temple at Amravati and Parvati Temple at Pune.

(*e*) The conference of the Mahars was convened at Dadar, Bombay on 30th and 31st May 1936 under the presidentship of B.S. Venkatrao, a Depressed Classes Leader from Hyderabad. Dr. Babasaheb Ambedkar addressed the mammth gathering. He said that, "you have nothing to lose, except your chains and everything to gain by changing your religion: Untouchability is a curse that has ruined your worldly existence, honour and name. I have decided once for all to give up this religion. My religious conversion is not inspired by any material motive.... Hinduism does not appeal to my conscience. My self respect can not assimilate Hinduism..... I tell you, religion is for man and not man for religion. If you want to organise, consolidate and be successful in this world, change this religion. The religion that does not recognise you as human beings, or give you water to drink, or allow you to enter the temples is not worthy to be called a religion. The religion that forbids you to receive education and comes in the way of your material advancement is not worthy of the appellation 'religion'... The religion that compels the ignorant to be ignorant and the poor to be poor is not religion but a visitation !" Lastly, he asked his followers, in the words of Buddha, that "to seek refuse in reason."[34] The conference declared by a resolution that they were prepared to change their religion and follow their leader.

His declaration to quit Hinduism had tremendous repercussions on the society in general and the Depressed Classes in particular. The Leaders of non-Hindu religions were very much optimistic and enthusiastic to receive the Depressed Classes in their faith, the Depressed Classes were very much eager to follow the path to be shown by their 'Babasaheb'. Even they started discarding Hindu way of life, Hindu deities, Hindu ethos and manners. However, Dr. Babasaheb Ambedkar, who was philosophically inclined to Buddhism, was busy with the comparative study of all the faiths and was seeking and observing the responses of his brethren throughout the country.

Dr. Babasaheb wanted to root out certain bad habits prevailing in the Depressed Classes which were to bring down the honour and self-pride of the Community: In a meeting organised in Mumbai on 16th June, 1936 Dr. Babasaheb Ambedkar advised the Devadasi, Murali *etc.,* to leave the unethical habits and disgraceful profession in the name of religion.[35]

He also advised his brethren in a meeting held at Pound in Pune district on 7-1-1937 that they should abandon eating beef and begging.[36] Further, he said at Solapur on 31-1-1937 that, they should wear a good-clean dress which would give a good appearance to them in the society.[37] He exhorted that they should revolt against tyranny of Caste Hindus. They should be free and fearless as they had nothing to lose in this battle.[38]

(f) Dr. Babasaheb Ambedkar thought religion should be based on principles and not on rules. He condemned a religion of rules. However, following Burke he thought that religion is the foundation of society. He had devised a plan to reform Hinduism so as to take it out from the priestly class and the rules formed by them. The following were the items in his plan of reform:

(i) There should be only one standard book of Hindu religion; acceptable to all Hindus.

(ii) The priesthood must cease to be hereditary. He must pass a prescribed examination and hold a sanad of priesthood.

(iii) The ceremony performed by a priest not holding the Sanad should be treated as invalid.

(iv) A priest should be subjected to disciplinary action by the state in the matter of morals, belief and worship.

(v) The number of priests should be limited.

(vi) Hinduism should be based on the new doctrine of liberty, equality and fraternity. It should be inconsonance with democracy. Hence, they have to discard the authority of the Shastras.

(vii) The Hindus must examine their religion and their morality in terms of their survival value.

(viii) The Hindus must consider whether they should conserve the whole of their social heritage or select what is helpful and worthy to transmit to future generation.

(ix) The Hindus must consider whether the time has not come for them to recognise that there is nothing fixed, nothing eternal, nothing Sanatan; that everything is changing, that change is the law of life for individuals as well as for society.

He said very categorically and explicitly that, "you must make your efforts to uproot caste, if not in my way, then in your way. I am sorry, I will not be with you. I have decided to change..... In my opinion only when the Hindu Society becomes a casteless society that it can hope to have strength enough to defend itself. Without such internal strength, *swaraj* for Hindus may turn out to be only a step towards slavery."[39]

(g) Speaking on the occasion of Buddha's birth anniversary in New Delhi, he said very categorically that the Buddha was a Teacher of Morality, he was neither God, nor the incarnation or messenger of God, but a Margadata, a wayfarer, a mere pathfinder. In his article, *"Buddha and the Future of his Religion"*, "contributed to the Mahabodhi Society's Journal, he laid down the true test of religion. He said, (1) The religion must be in accord with reason or science. (2) Its moral code should recognize the fundamental tenets of liberty, equality and fraternity. (3) It should be based on a moral code and (4) It should not sanctify or ennoble poverty. He thought that Buddhism fulfils the test of a true religion. Eventually, he declared on 5th May 1950 at Bombay, that he was defintely inclined to Buddhism. He went to Colombo to participate in Buddhist conference on 25th May 1950. Later, he went to Rangoon (Brahmadesh) to participate in the Buddhist conference held on 4th December 1954. He inauguarated the Buddha Vihar at Dehu Road, Pune and installed the Buddha statue presented to him in his Rangoon Conference. He founded the Buddhist Society of India at Bombay on 4th May 1955 to preach and propogate Buddhism in India. He visited Agra and inaugurated Buddha Vihar, at Chakkipat, Agra. He completed writing *'Buddha and His Dhamma'* in February 1956; and its preface on 15th March 1956. He ultimately declared on 24th March 1956 at Bombay that he would embrace Buddhism in October 1956 on the occasion of Vijayadashami Day.

As decided earlier, the Deeksha Initiation ceremony was organised on very largescale at Nagpur on 14th

October 1956 on the occasion of Ashok *Vijayadashmi* Day. It was officiated by Rev.Chandramuni. It was attended by other dignitories including D. Valisinh, on behalf of Maha Bodhi Society of India. On this occasion Dr. Babasaheb Ambedkar, Savita Ambedkar, Yeshwantrao alias Bhaiya Saheb Ambedkar, Nanak Chandu Rathu, Shankaranand Shastri, Justice Niyogi and many others embraced Buddhism. Dr. Babasaheb Ambedkar gave *Deeksha* to his millions of followers and addressed them. On 16th October, 1956 he went to Chandrapur and gave *Deeksha* to his followers.

Later on he went to Nepal to participate in the Fourth Conference of the World Fellowship of Buddhists to be held at Khatmandu. It was inaugurated by King Mahendra and presided over by Dr. Malalasekhara. Dr. Babasaheb Ambedkar made his thought-provoking speech on "Buddha and Karl Marx" on 20th November 1956.

Thus, his struggle for emancipation from all ignorance, untouchability and oppression came to its logical conclusion with the conversion to Buddhism. Probably, it might be the biggest ever programme in the human history which witnessed an innumerable mass of people embraced a religion at a time. He gave to his followers not a traditional religion, but a rational Buddhism in its proper perspective. It was but a code of moral principles useful for the development of the human beings.

2. Labour Welfare Legislation

Dr. Babasaheb Ambedkar was graciously nominated by the government of Bombay as a member of the Bombay Legislative Council with effect from 28th February 1927. He was nominated firstly from 1927 to 1932 for a period of five years and secondly from 1932 to 1937 for a period of another five years to the Bombay Legislature.

Apart from agitating against Untouchability, and caste–System, he endeavoured for the benefit of the toiling masses including the untouchables, labourers and small farmers.

(a) Agricultural Labour Welfare

(i) *On Small Holders Relief Bill*:

The Small Holders Relief Bill was introduced in the Legislative Council to solve two problems which affected the agriculturists of the Bombay Presidency; they were:

(1) the problem of scattered farms and other

(2) was the problem of small farms

While speaking on the Bill on 10th October 1927 Dr. Babasaheb Ambedkar admitted that a great many disadvantages in having scattered farms are being faced by the farmers and therefore such farms should be consolidated. However, he did not admit that small farms are necessarily uneconomic. He however thought that whether the farm is economic or uneconomic does not necessarily depend upon the size of the farm. It depends on other factors of production, such as labour, and capital. In order to solve the problem of small farms, he thought that, "The better method is to introduce co-operative agriculture for standard areas and to compel owners of small strips included therein to join in cultivation without destroying private ownership.[40] "The co-operative farm will be like a share holders company in which the company remains even though the shareholders change."[41] Thus, he was a strong protagonist of the co-operative farming or collective farming for the purpose of profitable production and equitable distribution of the yield.

As a member of the Bombay Legislative Council, he introduced the Bill No. XII of 1928 to amend the Bombay Hereditary Offices Act 1874, on 19th March, 1928.

According to Dr. Babasaheb, *The Mahar Watan*, was, " The most ancient and "an atrocious system" imposed on the inferior officers belonging to "The Mahars in the Deccan, the Vethias or the Varthanias in Gujarat, the Ramoshis or the Juglias and the Holiyas in Karnataka." The inferior servants were De Jure Government Servants, under the Bombay Hereditary Offices Act, 1874. However, due to want of definition of inferior servants, they were called upon to render services to almost all the government departments as the most inferior servants. If the head of the family of such servant was absent, any member irrespective of age or sex, was to serve the superior visiting officers".

Before introducing the Bill he tried to acquaint his community the object and contents of the proposed bill. A big Conference of the Watandar Mahars was convened at Kamathipura, Bombay on 5th November, 1927 under the Presidentship of R.B.S.K. Bole. It was reportedly attended by 5000 Watandar Maharas. Another conference of Watandar Mahars was held at Jalgaon on 13th November, 1927. He demanded that Watan lands should be given to the holders of land at the full rate of assessment, and they should be relieved from the obligation to serve the villagers and the officials. They were to get very marginal remuneration from two sources :

(1) The produce from the Inam Land and

(2) The Baluta, *i.e.,* The collection of grain made by the Watandar Mahars or Servants from the village. Moreover, their hours of work were not fixed. They were required to work or render services to the private parties in the villages and the Government Officials as and when they were to visit the village.

In order to do away with such an oppressive system of inferior service, Dr. Babasaheb Ambedkar proposed through the said Bill, that "The Watan Lands should be given to the holders of those posts at the full rate of assessment, and they should be relieved from the obligation to serve."[42]

Dr. Babasaheb Ambedkar wanted to give freedom of contract to the ryots as well as to the Mahars and other inferior servants to form the contract of service. He said that, "I think at least in this country when every society has advanced from status to contract we ought not for instance to block the progress of Indian Society by refusing the Mahars and the ryots the liberty of contract."[43]

However, due to want of majority support he was constrained to withdraw the Bill, on 24th July 1929.

(*ii*) *Bill No. XX to Abolish the Khoti System*:

Dr. Babasaheb Ambedkar was against feudalism and landlordism due to their inherent exploitative and oppressive nature. The *Khoti* system was "one of the minor land tenures" prevailing in Ratnagiri, Kolaba and Thana districts of the Bombay Presidency. The Khoti Tenure differs from the ordinary Rayatwari Tenure in as much as in the latter the Government collects revenue directly from those who are in occupation of the land while in the former the Government is required to employ the services of the *Khot* for the purpose of collecting revenue.[44] In the Ratnagiri district it was regulated by Bombay Act, 1 of 1880, in the Kolaba district it was regulated by Custom and Usage, and in the Thana district by grant.

In order to abolish the exploitative and hegemonic Khoti System Dr. Babasaheb Ambedkar introduced the Bill No. XX to Abolish the Khoti System on 17th September, 1937. The Bill aimed:

(i) "to abolish the Khoti System and to establish direct relationship between Government and those who are in possession or occupation of the land which is under the management or beneficial enjoyment of the Khot.

(ii) to make provision for the payment of reasonable compensation to the Khot for the loss of his rights, and

(iii) to give those inferior holders who are in actual occupation of the land the status of occupants within the meaning of the Land Revenue Code, and

(iv) to provide for other incidental purposes."[45]

The origin of the problem was in the system of payment of revenue by the inferior holders to the land lord. The collection of revenue from the inferior holders was the responsibility of the Khot. The Khot was free to collect or not to collect the revenue, but while imposing or collecting the revenue he allowed some concessions to the inferior holders and in exchange of that concesion, he subjected them to all kinds of exactions, which reduced them to a state of abject slavery.'[46]

The Bill to abolish the Khoti System was "a maiden attempt to initiate Legislative measures for the abolition of the Khoti System and it also satisfied the aspirations of the farmers as evoked during the election campign of February 1937. It proved that the ILP was true to its salt and the farmers realised afresh the ILP as their true spokesman."[47]

(iii) *Bill No. XXIII to Amend the Bombay Hereditary Offices Act, 1874*:

Dr. Babasaheb Ambedkar was very much determined to abolish the hereditary servitude of the untouchables, especially of the Mahars. When he was elected to the Bombay Legislative Assembly in 1937 as a member of Independent Labour Party which he himself founded, he introduced *Bill No. XXIII to Amend the Bombay Hereditary Offices Act, 1874* on 17th September 1937; on the line of the Bill which he introduced in 1928. The main object of this Bill was to free the Watandar from the liability to serve as a watandar without involving a loss to his right to the land which formed part of his watan. He said, that, "while it allows such a watandar to retain the land, it does not involve any loss to Government because Government will be entitled to recover from him full survey assessment."[48] It gives the right to watandars who were required to perform certain services as village servants to apply to the concerned Collector to convert payment in kind which they were to receive as remuneration into payment in money and requires the collector to convert the same in its money equivalent. Moreover, it gives the collector the Power in cases where the remuneration of the Watandar is a joint payment for services to Government as well as to the ryots to decide how much of it for services to Government and how much is for services to the ryots. The Bill was however not passed. Eventually, Mahar Watan was abolished under the Bombay Inferior village Watan Abolition Act of 1959.

A conference of the Watandar Mahars and Mangs was called at Haregaon, Taluka Kopargaon District Ahmednagar, on 16th December 1939. It was held under the presidentship of Dr. Babasaheb Ambedkar and it was attended by almost all the ILP members of the Legislative Assembly.

The Mahar–Mang Watandars were not getting adequate Baluta for their livelihood. Besides the Government was collecting the *'Judi'* in the form of grains on the Watan Land. This was oppressive and tortious on the part of Watandars - inferior village servants. Even the Revenue Department of the Bombay Government increased various duties and responsibilities of the Watandars to 19, vide a Resolution dated 13-9-1938. Therefore, the conference of the Watandar Mahars was convened to raise the voice against the Judi and increased duties of the Watandars. The conference, however passed the resolution against the *Judi* and increased duties and decided to submit a Memorandam to the Governor of the Bombay Presidency for getting relief from the said oppressive system. The memorandum to that effect was submitted to the Governor. Again Dadasaheb Gaikwad also tried to get the demands of the ILP approved. It seems that even Dr. Babasaheb Ambedkar also submitted an appeal to the Governor on 14th July 1941. Eventually, the Government had accepted to ban the *Judi* or additional tax on Watan Land.[49]

After seeking advice and moral support from Dr. Babasaheb Ambedkar, the Leaders and followers of Marathwada region of the then Hyderabad State launched a massive *Satyagraha* throughout the region for the distribution of the uncultivated or waste land for agricultural purpose to the landless peasants, mostly including the Scheduled Castes and Scheduled Tribes in 1953. The *Satyagraha* led by Dadasaheb Gaikwad (Nasik) and B.S. More (Aurangabad). The Satyagrahis about 1700 were arrested, however 1,100 were released unconditionally. It was withdrawn in November 1953 on the assurance given by the Government to consider the genuine demands of the Landless farmers.

(iv) *On Maternity Benefits Bill:*

The important Bill proposing maternity benefits for women labourers was introduced in the House. While supporting the Bill, Dr. Babasaheb Ambedkar emphatically said on 28th July 1928, that, it was in the interests of the nation that the mother ought to get a certain amount of rest during the pre-natal period with leave. He was of the opinion that it was in fact responsibility of the state, but he said that the employer who employs a woman can not be free from the liability of such benefit in the interests of the women.[50] The Bill was, however applicable to the women working in factories and not to other industries or to the agricultural occupation. It was said that in the factories the women are exposed to somewhat more dangers then the agricultural and other occupations.

(b) Industrial Worker's Welfare

(i) Railway Worker's Conference, Manmad:

The followers of Dr. Babasaheb Ambedkar organised a big conference of the Depressed Class Railway workers at Manmad in the Nasik District on February 12 and 13, 1938. The conference was the first of its kind. He said very rightly that, "there were two enemies of the working classes in the country and they were Brahmanism and Capitalism. By Brahmanism I mean the negation of the spirit of liberty, equality and fraternity. In that sense it is rampant in all classes and is not confined to Brahmins alone though they have been its originators. The effects of Brahmanism were not confined only to social rights such as inter dining and inter-marrying. It denied them also the civic rights. So omniscient is Brahmanism that it even affects the field of economic opportunities.".... "He observed that it was notorious that there were many appointments from which a Depressed Class Worker was shut out by reason of the fact that he was an untouchable. "Eventually, he told the workers that they must uproot Brahmanism, the spirit of inequality from among the workers, if the ranks of labour were to be united..... He proceeded, after the disappearance of imperialism, labour would require to fight the landlords, mill owners and money lenders who would remain in India to bleed the people, it should have its own organisation from the moment to fight capitalism as much as imperialism."[51] The conference was very successfully organised, it continued for two days and attended by nearabout twenty thousand workers from all over the country.

(ii) On Industrial Dispute Bill of 1938 (Bill No.XXI of 1938)

The said Bill was presented by the then Congress Government. The purpose of the Bill was to replace the Bombay Trade Disputes Conciliation Act of 1934. It provided for voluntary conciliation of the trade dispute.

Presently, the Industrial Dispute Bill proposed compulsory conciliation. Other provisions of the Bill were regarding strikes which were equally controversial. Therefore, the Independent Labour Party opposed the provisions of the Industrial Dispute Bill. The present Bill proposed strike under certain conditons as illegal. It was stated under clause 62 (1) of the Bill that, "A strike shall be illegal if it is commenced or continued".

(a) In cases where it relates to any industrial matter mentioned in Schedule 1, before the standing orders relating to such matter and submitted to the Commissioner of Labour Under Section 26 are settled by him or by the Industrial Court, as the case may be or before the expiry of one year from the date on which such standing orders come into operation under Section 26.

(b) Without giving notice in accordance with the provisions of Section 28.

(c) Only for the reasons that the employer has not carried out the provisions of any standing order or has made an illegal change.

(d) In cases where notice of the change is given in accordance with the provisions of Section 28 and where no agreement in regard to such change is arrived at, before the statement of the case referred to in Section 34 is received by the Registrar.

(e) In cases where conciliation proceedings in regard to the industrial dispute to which the strike relates have commenced, before the completion of such proceedings.

(f) In cases where submission relating to such dispute or such kind of dispute is registered under Section 43, until such submission is lawfully revoked; or

(*g*) In contravention of the terms of registered agreement, settlement or award.

(2) In cases where conciliation proceedings in regard to any industrial dispute have been completed, a strike relating

to such dispute shall be illegal if it is commenced at any time after the expiry of two months after the completion of such proceedings."

In order to make this clause effective, the Bill prescribes certain strigent penalties for indulging in such illegal strikes. According to Dr. Babasaheb Ambedkar, to penalise a strike, therefore, 'was nothing short of making the worker a slave' as such it was "contrary to ethic."[52] Thus, he opposed to the Bill. The Independent Labour Party alongwith all the opposition parties observed one day strike on 7th November, 1938 to mark their protest against the said Bill.

(3) Dr. Babasaheb Ambedkar had got a very noteworthy opportunity to be labour member in the Viceroy's Executive Council from 20th July 1942 to the end of June 1946. After his appointment he gave an assurance to the working class that, "I shall not surrender in the battle I will have to wage for protecting and advancing the interests of the working class in India in the Executive Council...."[53]

(iii) The major functions performed by the Ministry of Labour headed by Dr. Babasaheb Ambedkar could be epitomised as under:

(1) *Formation of the Indian labour conference and the standing labour committee*: The Indian Labour Conference was a Tripartite Body consisting of representatives of the employers, representatives of the employees and representatives of the Government. The object of this organisation was to establish harmonious industrial relations in India.

(2) *Standing Labour Committee*: It was established to monitor the implementation of the decisions of the Tripartite Labour Conference.

(3) *Central Industrial Relations Machinery*: The Central Industrial Relations Machinery was formed on 9th April 1945 consisting of the following:

(i) A Chief Labour Commissioner (Central) with Head Quarters at New Delhi.

(ii) Three Regional Labour Commissioners (Central) with Head Quarters at Bombay, Calcutta and Lahore.

(ii) A Deputy Labour Commissioner (H.Q.) at New Delhi.

(iv) Nine Conciliation Offices and 23 Labour Inspectors (Central) located at various Centres throughout India.

(v) One Central Inspector of Industrial Concerns.

The central industrial relations machinery was "charged with the duties of prevention and settlement of industrial disputes enforcement of labour laws and promotion of labour welfare in the industries and undertakings controlled by the Central Government, the then federal railways and in mines, oil-fields and major ports."[54]

(4) *Progress of Labour Legislation in India*: (1942 to 1946)

The Laws relating to Labour Welfare and Security during 1942 to 1946 are listed as under:

Acts proposed to be amended or newly made	*Amendment or Act to be made*	*Purpose of Amendment or Act*
1943:		
1. The Indian Boilers Act, 1923 (29th July 1943)	The Indian Boilers Amendment Act, 1943 (Section 28)	Obligatory upon the inspector to examine Steam-boilers and also feed pipies.
2. The Motor Vehicles (Divers) Ordinance, 1942 (29th July 1943)	The Motor Vehicle Amendment Act, 1943	Facilitating reemployment of Drivers
3. The Mines Maternity	The Mines	Maternity benefit for

Benefit Act, 1941 (29th July 1943)	Maternity Benefit (Amendment) Act, 1943	Four Weeks preceding the delivery and four weeks after the delivery with pay.
1944:		
1. Coal Mines Labour Welfare Ordinance, 1944 (15th February 1944)		Constituting a Fund to promote the Welfare of Labour employed in the Coal-Mining Industry and Advisory Committee
2. The Coal Mines Safety (Stowing) Act, 1939 (23rd February 1944)	The Coal Mines Safety Amendment Bill 1944 (Section 8)	Permits the Board to take necessary steps for safety.
3. The Factories Act, 1934.	The Factories (Amendment) Act, 1944 (9,19,23,45 and 54)	Inspector of Factories Empowered to Collect information from factories and to provide compensatory holiday to the Workers.
1945:		
1. The Mines Maternity Benefit Act, 1941 (11 April 1945)	The Mines Maternity (Benefit) Amendment Act, 1945	A woman has to satisfy the condition that she worked for 90 days under ground within the period of six months prior to delivery she would get Rs. six a week maternity benefit
1946:		
1. The Workmen's Compensation Act, 1923 (8th February 1946)	The Workmen Compensation Act, 1946.	Protecting the workmen by raising the monthly wages (from 300-400)
2. The Indian Mines Act, 1923	Indian Mines (Amendment)	Pit-head baths should be provided

	(8th February 1946)	Act, 1946	by the Colliery Owners
3.	Industrial Employment (Standing Orders) Bill 12th April 1946.		The Bill required the employees to define conditions of employment
4.	Mica Mines Labour Welfare Fund Bill (15th April 1946)		Obligation upon the owner of the Mica Mines to Constitute Mica Mines Labour Fund for Providing Certain Facilities such as Urinals and Latrines,Washing and Drinking Water, Dwelling facilities etc.
5.	The Indian Trade Unions Act, 1926	Indian Trade Unions (Amendment) Bill, 1946	Regarding recognition of Trade Unions. (It was however less passed in 1947)

3. Educational Thought and Institutions

Dr. Babasaheb Ambedkar has rightly thought that education is a *sine quo non* of the development of human beings. He said very categorically that, "coming as I do from the lowest order of the Hindu Society, I know what is the value of education. The problem of raising the lower order is deemed to be economic. This is a great mistake. The problem of raising the lower order in India is not to feed them, to clothe them and to made them serve the higher order as is the ancient ideal of this country. The problem of lower order is to remove from that inferiority complex which has stunted their growth and mate them slaves to others, to create in them the consciousness of the significance of their lives for themselves and for the country of which they have been cruelly robbed by the existing social order. Nothing can achieve this purpose except the spread of higher education. This is, in my opinion, the panacea of our social troubles."[55] Therefore, he gave a dictum, "Educate, agitate and organise." (1924). He was of the view that, the State, which is a welfare state in democracy, must take a lead in spreading education and must see that it is in the reach of the common man.

He was aware of the fact that due to ignorance and utmost poverty the Depressed Classes people were reluctant and unable to send their children to the School. Hence, he secured post-matric scholarship to the Scheduled Castes in 1944, and to the Scheduled Tribes in 1948 for facilitating higher education to the weaker strata of the society.

While speaking on the grants for education in the Bombay Legislative Council on 12th March 1927, he said that the Government was spending very meagre amount on education, as such it should increase the grants to be given to the schools. He argued that "favoured treatment to those who are below the level" should be given.

He founded "Depressed Classes Education Society," in 1928 itself, and started six hostels for the Depressed Classes each one, at Sholapur, Panvel, Thane, Pune, Nasik and Dharwad in the erstwhile Bombay State. The students were provided with free boarding and lodging facilities and books. The hostels did a Yeoman Service in promoting primary and High School Education amongst the untouchable communities."[56]

Later on, he founded the People's Education Society, at Bombay on 8th July 1945 to spread education among the poor strata of the society. The society had established various educational institutions in his life time. They are as under:

1. Siddharth College of Arts and Science (1946);
2. Siddharth Night School (1947);
3. Siddharth College of Commerce and Economics (1953);
4. Siddharth College of Law (1956), (all at Mumbai)
5. Milind Mahavidyalaya (1950); (Arts, Science and Commerce College)
6. Milind Multi-purpose High school (1955), (both at Aurangabad)

4.Political Mission

(*a*) *On Representation of the Scheduled Castes*:

Where a dominant communal majority and the divergent communal minorities perpetually exist, some method of due representation needs to be devised. Separate electorate is one of the best methods of achieving adequate and effective representation of the minorities in the decision-making bodies. Therefore, a method of separate electorate was introduced in respect of the Muslims under the Act of 1909. It was extended to the Sikhs and Europeans in 1919, and to the Indian Christians and Anglo-Indians under the Act of 1935. Dr. Babasaheb Ambedkar, who was equally eager to secure due and effective representation in the legislature made the demand of separate electorate to the Scheduled Castes in 1919, before the South Borough Franchise Committee. In his report submitted to the Simon Commission, he demanded adult franchise and Joint-electorates with reserved seats for almost all the communities except the Europeans. While giving evidence before the Simon Commission in 1928, he replied to a question, "if there is no adult franchise?" saying that, "then we would ask for separate electorates."[57]

In order to decide the nature of future Constitution and Settle the communal problem, the British Government convened the Round Table Conference in London consisting of the representatives of India, the British Government and the British Political Parties, on November 12, 1930. It met under the presidentship of Ramsay Mac Donald, the Prime-Minister of England. The conference was adjourned on 19th January 1931. The Second Round Table Conference began on 17th September, 1931. It was adjourned on 1st December 1931. The British government, however conceded the demand of separate electorate made by Dr. Babasasheb Ambedkar and Rao B.R. Srinivasan, under the

Communal Award; but due to antagonistic attitude of Mahatma Gandhi in that respect, he had to relinquish it and accept Joint-electorates with reserved seats under the Poona - Pact, 1932. The Third Round Table Conference was convened on 17th November 1932 to confirm and finalise the minutes of the previous conferences. It adjourned on 4th December 1932.

Text of the Poona-Pact, 1932

(1) There shall be seats reserved for the Depressed Classes out of the general electorates seats in the Provincial Legislatures as follows[58] :

Madras	.....	30
Bombay with Sind	.....	15
Punjab	.....	8
Bihar and Orissa	....	18
Central Provinces	....	20
Assam	....	7
Bengal	....	30
United Provinces	....	20
Total	....	**148**

(2) *Elections to these seats shall be by joint electorates*:

However, the Scheduled Castes Voters will elect a panel of four candidates belonging to the Depressed Classes for each of such reserved seats, the four getting the highest number of votes in each such primary election shall be candidates for election by the general electorate.

(3) In the Central Legislature, eighteen per cent of seats shall be reserved for the Depressed Classes.

(4) The election shall be on the principle of joint electorates and reserved seats according to the procedure followed in the Provincial Legislatures.

(5) The system of primary election to a panel of candidates shall come to an end after the first ten years.

(6) The system of representation of the 'Depressed Clases' shall continue until determined by mutual agreement between the communities concerned in the settlement.

(7) The franchise for Central and Provincial Legislatures shall be as indicated in the Lothian Committee Report.

(8) Appointment to the Public Services and Local bodies shall be made subject to such educational qualifications as laid down.

(9) In every province educational facilities shall be provided to the Depressed Classes Students.

Although the Poona-Pact was not fully advantageous to the Depressed Classes, Dr. Babasaheb had to accept it as a matter of amicable compromise in that diabolitical and crucial period. He said very categorically that the Poona-Pact was "fraught with mischief". It was accepted because of the coercive fast of Mahatma Gandhi and because of the assurances given at the time that the Hindus will not interfere in the election of the Scheduled Castes.[59] It was, thus a product of unusual situation for which there was no alternative. It can be said, in the words of G.W. Johnson, that "a man cannot be held responsible for acting in one way unless he is free to act in another way."[60]

(b) *Independent Labour Party*:

With the passage of the Government of India Act 1935, by the British Government a new era of Politics was ushered in India. Dr. Babasaheb Ambedkar, who gave prime importance to political power for the liberation of the Depressed Classes formed the Independent Labour Party on 15th August 1936, and started the political activities with a new vigour. Dr. Babasaheb Ambedkar was its President and Treasurer; Shri M.B. Samarth was its Secretary and K.V. Chitre and S.A. Upshyam Guruji were its Joint Secretaries. It was open to all the Castes and Communities; Peasants and Labourers.

(1) The ILP stood for representative and responsive government. It promised to secure the separation of the judiciary from the executive. It promised to give fair opportunity to all the castes and communities in the administration.

(2) In order to abolish money lending by the private money-lenders, it proposed to open financial agencies like land mortgage Banks Co-operative Credit Societies and Marketing Societies.

(3) It promised to protect agricultural tenants from the exactions and evictions by the landlords, especially the khots and talukdars.

(4) The party thought that fragmentation of holdings was a 'Severe Handicap' in the development of agriculture. Hence, it proposed to establish co-operative societies for the agricultural purpose.

(5) In order to improve the economic condition of the industrial workers, it promised to make laws to fix hours of work, adequate wages, leave with wages, and to provide cheap and sanitary dwellings for the workers.

(6) It promised to promote industries. Even it thought to apply the principles of state management and state ownership of industry in the interests of the workers.

(7) It proposed to provide free and compulsory primary education and adult education.

(8) The party proposed to undertake for all necessary social reforms and for preventing social boycott. It promised to amend the 'watan' system in a way suited to modern conditions.[61]

The ILP contested 20 seats (13 reserved and 7 general seats) for the Bombay Provincial Assembly. It also contested 15 seats (10 reserved and 5 general seats) for the C.P. and Berar Assembly.

The elections were held on 17th February 1937. Due to its labour oriented and popular programme and the able leadership, the party won 14 seats in Bombay

Presidency (11 reserved and 3 general seats) and 7 seats in C.P. and Berar on Reserved Seats. Besides, two members were nominated by the Governor to the Bombay Legislative Council.

The role played by ILP in the Politics of Bombay Presidency and the C.P. and Berar and in the National Politics is of grate importance. That could be summarised as under:

(1) *Political Contribution*: Dr. Babasaheb Ambedkar did not like the idea of the Federation envisaged under the Act of 1935. He thought that India ought to be free from the slavery of princedom and bureaucracy.

Dr. Babasaheb Ambedkar gave his support to the British in their war against the AXIS countries. However, he thought that, "it was unfair to India that it should have no voice in her foreign policy in declaring war and in the making of peace."[62]

When Jinnah decided to observe 22nd December 1939 as a 'Deliverance Day' after the Congress Ministries had resigned in seven Provinces in the wake of the Britisher's unilateral declaration of India's participation in World War-II, Babasaheb Ambedkar, who was equally antagonistic to Congress and Hindu Raj, decided to observe the 'Deliverance, Day and acted accordingly.

Dr. Babasaheb Ambedkar could successfully convince the British Government to start recruitment of the Mahars into a separate regiment. In view of the valient tradition of the Mahars and exigencies of the war, the British Government raised the 1st Battalion of the Mahar Regiment on 1st October 1941.

(2) *Economic Contribution:* The role of the ILP in the economic affairs was of immense importance. On 17th September 1937, Dr. Babasaheb Ambedkar introduced a Bill in the Legislative Assembly of the Bombay Presidency to abolish the Khoti System of Land Tenure (an exploitative serfdom of agricultural tenants) prevailing

in the Konkon region. It aimed at abolishing the Khoti System with a view to securing occupancy rights to the Tenants. The Bill contemplating the same was introduced by S.C. Joshi, ILP member, in the Legislative Council. A huge march of peasants was organised on 10th January 1938 to protest against the Khoti System and submitted a memorandum of demands on behalf of the agricultural tenants.

Dr. Babasaheb Ambedkar, leader of the ILP convened the Railway Workers' Conference at Manmad on February 12 and 13, 1938, where he said that, "There were two enemies of the working classes in the country and they were Brahminism and capitalism."[63]

(3) *Social Affairs*: Dr. Babasaheb Ambedkar gave priority to social reforms. He aimed to reconstruct the society on the principles of "liberty, equality and fraternity."

He thought to liberate the so-called untouchable castes from the involuntary servitude imposed by the Brahmanic forces and preserved by the Hindu Tradition. He thought that the Mahar Watan (the hereditary bonded service system imposed by the Brahmanic forces on the Maharas—an untouchable community in Maharashtra) was a major stumbling bloc in the way of progress of the Mahars. Hence, he introduced a Bill to abolish the Mahar Watan, on 17th September 1937 in the Bombay Legislative Assembly. The same was introduced by S.C. Joshi in the Legislative Council. However, it was not passed at that time. It was eventually abolished under the Bombay Inferior village Watan Abolition Act, 1959.

The ILP, member Shri P.J. Roham moved a resolution on 10th November 1938 in the Legislative Assembly to recommend to the Government for taking necessary steps in respect of birth control, but in vain.

There were serveral other Bills and proposals on which the ILP members expressed their well-considered views and observations, such as, Bills regarding primary and university education Panchayat Raj and local boards, prohibition, independence of the judiciary etc,.

However, with the declaration of India's participation in the Second World War by the British Government political activity in India came to standstill till the end of war.

(c) *All India Scheduled Castes Federation*:

The declaration of India's participation in Wrold War II, by the British Government caused much resentment in India. In order to deal with the matter and seek the co-operation of the people of India, the British Government sent Sir Stafford Cripps to India in March 1942. It was declared by Cripps that India was to get freedom after the end of the war and an elected body to frame the new Constitution would be formed. The provinces of British India, as well as the Indian States, were allowed to have the option to join the Union of India. Thus, Cripps unequivocally accepted the demand of the Muslim League for the formation of Pakistan. Cripps, however, took care to appease Hindus as well as Muslims, but did not take care to take cognizance of the Scheduled Castes. Therefore, Babasaheb Ambedkar expressed his resentment over the proposals declared by Cripps; saying that, it is "a breach of faith and a sudden volte face."[64] Hence, he was naturally constrained to intensify the Dalit movement under a separate political party.

Ultimately, he convened a meeting of his followers all over the country to discuss the Cripps proposals and the formation of a national level political party at Nagpur on 17-20th July 1942. Under the initiative of Dr. Babasaheb Ambedkar an All India Scheduled Castes Federation was unanimously formed in the mammoth gathering. An executive body of the all India SCF was elected in the Convention. N. Shivraj was elected President and P.N. Roybhoj was elected as General Secretary. The other members of the SCF were: R.L. Biswas, J.N. Mandal, Roy Dhuria (Bengal), D.G. Jadhav,

Dadasaheb Gaikwad (Bombay) Gopal Singh, Seth Kishan Das (Punjab) Revaram Kawade, Shendre, Kosare (C.P. and Berar) Raosaheb Shyamlal, Walmiki, Babu Tilakchand (U.P.) and Shri Wodapally (Madras).

It was, however not a Political Party of a Specific Caste or Sub-caste. It was open to all the Scheduled Castes, which were around four hundred. It was, thus a party of all the deprived castes in India.[65]

In March 1946, general elections for the Provincial Assemblies were held. The SCF, like other Political Parties, participated in the elections. It contested altogether 51 seats (Madras 24, Bombay 5, Bengal 6, U.P.5. C.P. and Berar-11). Of all the contestants only one candidate from Bengal (J.N. Mandal), and another candidate from C.P. and Berar (Raibhan Jadhav) were elected.

The British Government with a view to giving full freedom to India and deciding the nature of the future Constitution, sent the Cabinet Mission to India on 24th March 1946 to hold discussions with the Indian Leaders. The representatives of the Congress, the Muslim League and the Hindu Mahasabha appeared before the Cabinet Mission to apprise it of their views. Dr. Babasaheb Ambedkar also appeared before the Cabinet Mission on behalf of the SCF, and submitted a Memorandam of various demands. However, the British Government did not concede the demands of the SCF. It was, of course, proposed, that there would be an Interim Government consisted of the Congress and the Muslim League. Both the major parties accepted the Cabinet Mission Plan.

Thereafter, in view of the apathetic attitude of the Cabinet Mission and the Congress towards the political rights of the Scheduled Castes, the SCF started a *Satyagraha* on 15th July 1946 at Poona under the leadership of P.N. Rajbhoj. Besides this, the *Satyagrahas* were launched at different places like Bombay, Nagpur, Kanpur, Lucknow, Calcutta etc; but it was of no avail.

The Interim Ministry was announced on 24th August 1946. It was consisted of five members from Congress, five members from the Muslim League and one each from Sikhs, Anglo-Indians, Parsis and Christians. There was, of course, no specific provision for inclusion of members of the Scheduled Castes. However, the Congress included Babu Jagjivan Ram, a Scheduled Caste member from Bihar in its ministry. The Muslim League which joined the Interim Ministry on 26th October 1946 had taken up Jogendra Nath Mandal SCF in its quota.

Subsequently, Dr. Babasaheb Ambedkar went to London in October 1946 and submitted a Memorandum of Demands to the British Prime Minister Mr. Atlee, The Secretary of State for India, Lord Pethick Lawrence and the Conservative Leader, Mr. Churchill, but in vain.

Meanwhile, elections to the Constituent Assembly were held. The members of the Constituent Assembly were elected by the members of the Provincial Assemblies. Dr. Babasaheb Ambedkar in view of want of supporters in other provinces, got elected from the SCF and Muslim League from Bengal Provincial Legislature. However, due to the partition of Bengal under the Indian Independence Act, the seat won by Babasaheb Ambedkar with great efforts was lost. Ultimately, the Congress Leaders realised his intelligence and integrity got him elected from the Bombay Provincial Legislature in July 1947.

The Constituent Assembly met on 9th December 1946 and elected Dr. Rajendra Prasad as its President on 11th December 1946. In March 1947, Dr. Babasaheb Ambedkar submitted a Memorandum to the Constituent Assembly which envisaged State-socialism, Parliamentry democracy and the special privilenges for the Scheduled Castes. It was published in the form of a broucher, under the title 'State and Minorities.'

Dr. Babasaheb Ambedkar was included in the first

cabinet of free India as Law Minister. On 29th August, 1947, he was elected Chairman of the Drafting Committee of the Constitutsent Assembly.

On 29th November 1948, the Constituent Assembly resolved to abolish untouchability. It was, however a Red Letter Day in the social history of India. The Constitution drafted by Dr. Babasaheb Ambedkar and adopted by the Constituent Assembly came into force on 26th January 1950.

Later on, he was constrained to resign from the Ministry on 27th September 1951 due to difference of opinion with Pandit Nehru on the complicated issues like allotment of the portfolio, the Kashmir issue, foreign policy, the Hindu code bill and the safeguards to the other backward classes. Once again he assumed the role of an opposition Leader.

The first General Elections under the new Constitution were held in January 1952. The SCF contested altogether 34 Lok Sabha Seats. (These were: four from Bombay, three from Central Provinces, nine from Madras, two from Punjab, eight from U.P., four from Hyderabad, one from Rajasthan, one from Delhi, one from Himachal Pradesh and one from Vindhya Pradesh). Out of them only two candidates were elected they were P.N. Rajbhoj from Solapur (R) and other was M.R. Krishna from Karimnagar. Even Dr. Babasaheb Ambedkar, who contested from Bombay (North) could not get elected. The SCF contested 215 seats for the legislative Assemblies of various states. Of all the 215 seats, the party won 12 seats. They were five from Hyderabad, two from Madras, one from Bomb ay, two from Mysore, one from Pepsu and one from H.P.

Dr. Babasaheb Ambedkar got elected from the Bombay Legislature to the Rajya Sabha in March 1952. J.H. Subhiah, The SCF leader from Hyderabad also got elected to the Rajya Sabha in 1952.

The role played by the SCF in Indian politics and social reforms is of immense importance. It could be epitomised as under:

(1) *Politico-legal Activites*: It could unite almost all the Scheduled Castes under the banner of SCF and enlist their participation in the field of politics. It could train them in propagating and protecting their interests by peaceful and constitutional means.

As a Law Minister, Babasaheb Ambedkar introduced several reform in the Hindu family known as Hindu Code. However, due to orthodox Brahmanic forces it was deliberately postponed. As a member of Rajya Sabha, he participated in the debates on many Bills. His speeches on the 'untouchability' (Offences) Bill and the Report of the Commissioner for Scheduled Castes and Scheduled Tribes of were specific importance.

(2) *Socio-economic Activities*: He could secure 8 1/3 per cent reservation in appointments for the Scheduled Castes in Aguust 1943. It is due to his efforts a special provision was made for the first time in the Central Budget in 1944 for the grant of Scholarships for the Scheduled Caste students. This facility was extended to the Scheduled Tribes in 1948.

The *Satyagraha* for uncultivated land by the landless labourers, especially the Scheduled Castes was launched in Marathwada region of then Hyderabad State in 1953 under the Leadership of Dadasaheb Gaikwad and B.S. More, the SCF Leaders. It became successful to a great extent.

[5] Contribution to the Indian Constitution

Dr. Babasaheb Ambedkar was a great legal philosopher and a great Jurist. He was honoured by the Constituent Assembly by electing him as Chairman of the Drafting Committee on 29th August 1947. As the architect of the Constitution, he was not only responsible for preparing its draft, but he enriched it with his Constitutional philosophy.

(i) *Written Constitution*: Indian Constitution is a deliberate creation of the leading men in India drawn from different fields and practical experience. The Drafting Committee consisting of Dr. Babasaheb Ambedkar (the hon'ble chairman) Alladi Krishnaswami Ayyar, N. Gopalswami Ayyangar, K.M. Munshi, Saiyid M. Sadulla, B.L. Mitter, (Later N. Madhav Rao) and D.P. Khaitan, (Later T.T. Krishnamachari), met firstly on 29th August 1947. It was to scrutinise and to suggest necessary amendment to the Draft Constituton of India prepared in the Office of the Assembly on the basis of the decision taken in the Assembly."[66] It was, however prepared by B.N. Rau, the Constitutional Advisor. It contained 243 Articles and 13 Schedules.

The Drafting Committee under the Chairmanship of Dr. Babasaheb Ambedkar considered the Preliminary Draft, Constituent Assembly debates, reports of various committees and sub-committees, public opinions and finalised the first draft of the Constitution, during 30th August 1947 to 21st February 1948. The first Draft of the Constitution consisted of 315 Articles and eight Schedules. The first Draft of the Constitution was before the Constituent Assembly till 26th November 1949 when it was unanimously adopted. In its final form it consisted of 395 Articles and nine Schedules. It came into implementation on 26th January 1950.

(ii) *Preamble to the Constitution*: Although the Preamble of the Constitution which contains the philosophy of the Constitution is based on Objectives Resolution but it is a great advance over the same. It has been embellished and ornamented with philosophical gems top to toe. It serves two purposes; one it discloses the source of authority and other, it states the objectives of the Constitution. It states that the Constitution has been ordained by "We, the People of India" who solemnly resolved to constitute India into a "Sovereign, Socialist, Secular, Democratic, Republic and pledged to secure to all its citizens, Justice"— social, economic, political, liberty of thought expression, belief, faith and worship, equality of status and opportunity and fraternity assuring the dignity of the "individual and unity and integrity of the nation." Every word of the preamble has been properly carved out and put in its proper perspective, on which the whole edifice of the Constitutional structure is based. It however gives prime importance to the objective of justice and it serves as a key to interpretation of the Constitution.

(iii) *A New Social Order*: The Constitution of India envisages a new social order totally different from the traditional one. In order to bring about socio-economic justice the Constitution under its Directive Principles of State Policy gives directive to the state to promote welfare of the people, to maintain a social order in which everybody would get justice; to provide for human conditions of work, living wages, early childhood care and welfare of the weaker sections of the society, and to promote international peace and security.

(iv) *Separation of Power*: The Constitution matains the theory of separation of power and maintains equilibrium among all the three branches of the government, executive, lagislative and judiciary. The President is the Head of the state. He is the Commander-in-Chief of the armed forces. He appoints the Prime Minister and his Cabinet. The Prime-Minister is head of the executive and responsible to the Parliament for his administration. The Parliament comprising the President, and two Houses of the legislatures are responsible for making laws, amending the laws and repealing the laws subject to judicial review. The Parliament is exclusively responsible for passing the Union Budget. Judiciary is expected to interpret the laws and statutes and to deliver the decisions. It is the duty of the judiciary to protect the Constitution in letter and spirit. The Supreme Court of India is the highest judicial authority. The Chief Justice of India and other judges are appointed by the President of India. They are removeable by impeachment motion by the Parliament. In accordance with Art.13 and Article 372 of the Constitution, "All Laws in force" before the commencement of the Constitution, in so far as they are inconsistent with the provisions of the Constitution, "shall to the extent of such inconsistency, be void." Moreover, the state can not make any law which goes against the principles and provisions of the Constitution. Thus, it marks a departure from the past Social Order and links with the ensuing social order based on liberty, equality, fraternity, rationality and humanity.

In its bid to restructure the society on egalitarian basis, it has pledged to minimise the rigours of caste and class society, bring gender equality, maintain communal harmony and bring socio-economic justice, especially to the weaker sections of the soceity, including the Scheduled Castes, Scheduled Tribes and Other Backward Classes.

It has envisaged Fundamental Rights to all the citizens irrespective of caste, creed, religion, sex, language and region: They are Right to equality, Right to freedom, Right against exploitation. Right to freedom of religion, Cultural and educational rights and Right to constitutional remedies. The weaker sections of the society got special safeguards and the minorities got the right to establish their own educational institutions.

(v) *Parliamentary form of Government*: We have adopted parliamentary form of Government. Prime Minister, who is head of the Council of Ministers is appointed by the President. Prime Minister is leader of the majority party in Parliament and enjoys confidence of the Parliament. He is collectively responsible and accountable to the Parliament. It is the duty of the Prime Minister "to aid and advise" The President in the execution of the State. The Parliament is empowered to amend the Constitution, subject to 'Basic Structure' of the Constitution and to make and unmake the Laws, subject to judicial review. Parliament being the representative body represents the public opinion and grievances of the people and ensures democratic government, However, it has got limited supremacy as compared to the British Parliament.

(vi) *Quasi-federal State*: Indian Constitution envisages a unique form of state. It is quasi-federal; neither fully unitary nor fully federal. Our Constitution fulfils all the essential elements of the federation like division of power among the union and the states, federal court, bicameral legislature and state autonomy. However, it also provides for centrally appointed Governors and High Court Judges, Election Commission, UPSC, Single Citizenship, Civil and Criminal Laws and Emergency Powers and Residuary Powers which are essential attributes of unitary form of government. The Federating Units are not the creation of an agreement, as such they cannot secede from the Union. Even their names and boundries are subject to change by the Union Government. Dr. Babasaheb Ambedkar was a protagonist of a strong unitary Government.

(vii) *Secular State*: In view of pluralistic character of Indian Scoiety, the Policy of Secularism is very much essential. The Constitution under its preamble and provisions of Fundamental Rights provides for the philosophy of secularism. It pledges "to secure to all its citizens liberty of faith, belief and worship. It guarantees to all persons equality before law and equal protection of laws irrespective of their caste, creed, sex, place of birth and religion. It States unequivocally that, "Subject to Public order morality and health all persons are equally entitled to freedom of conscience and the right freely to profess, practice and propagate religion. The religious minorities are free to conserve their language and culture. People may have their own religion or no religion, but the state has no religion. No religious instruction would be provided in any educational institution wholly maintained out of state funds. It is the bounden duty of every citizen to maintain communal order, peace and security in the society.

(viii) *Special Safeguards to the Weaker Sections*: The Scheduled Castes, Scheduled Tribes and Other Backward Classes who suffered a lot due to *'untouchability'*, tribalism and social and educational backwardness respectively were in need of special safeguards for their upliftment. Therefore, they are entitled to avail facilities under Article 15(4) and Article 16(4) and Article 46 of the Constitution. The Scheduled Castes and the Scheduled Tribes are entitled to avail political reservation under Articles 330 and 332 of the Constitution for a certain period.

(*ix*) *Procedure of Amendment*: The procedure of amendment has been given under Article 368 of the Constitution. Accordingly, the Constitution would be amended by:

(a) Simple majority certain minor changes could be effected *e.g.*, the names and boundries of the States, Salaries, Allowances etc., of the President, Governors, Judges of the Supreme Court and High Court etc.

(b) Special majority, means by a majority of the total membership of the house and by a majority of not less than two-thirds of the members present and voting certain amendments could be done;

(c) If the amendment is in respect of Presidential electoral college, extent of the executive Powers of the Union and the States, Jurisdiction of the Supreme Court and the High Courts, representation of the states in Parliament and the amending procedure itself, then it requires ratification by at least 50 per cent of the State Legislatures. Thereafter, the Bill is presented to the President and after his assent, the Constitution stands amended as per terms of the Bill. Due to this simple as well as complicated method, it is said that the Constitution is rigid as well as flexible. Till now it has accommodated more than hundred amendments to the Constitution. Thus the

Parliament in its Constituent power can amend any part of the Constitution subject to the 'Basic Structure' theory enunciated subsequently.

(x) *Instrument of Socio-economic Transformation*: The Constitution of India is a prime document ensuring the fulfilment of the aspirations of the people. From 1950 till now, it has not only sustained the difficult upheavals but it contributed much by its philosophy and provisions to the overall development of the people in general and the backward classes in particular. Our socio-economic, scientific and technological progress and our status in the global community could be attributed to the Constitutional Values and Provisions of the Constitution. Although there was no provision of 'Socialism' in Part IV of the Constitution, Babasaheb Ambedkar said very categorically that, "If these directive principles to which I have drawn attention are not socialistic in their direction and in their content, I fail to understand what more socialism can be."[67] He provided the agenda of socialism in the Constitution without using the word in express terms.

Conclusion

In order to liberate the exploited proletariat, Karl Marx found a new philosophy of Scientific-Socialism or Communism. He was not merely a thinker but an activists to the core. He tried to spread communism through out the world by inspiring directly or through writings and by setting up Communist organisations.

Babasaheb Ambedkar also tried to emancipate the untouchables, tribals, backwards and women from their ignorance and *Shastras*. He gave them Buddhism, a philosophy based on liberty, equality, fraternity and rationality. He gave the Constitution to "We, the People of India" and through the Constitution, he gave *inter-alia*, justice, liberty, equality and fraternity. It is his philosophy of social justice, which is leading India to silent revolution.

Notes and References

1. Marx-Engels: *Manifesto of the Communist Party*, p. 96. Peoples Publishing House, New Delhi. (2012).
2. DBAWS.Vol. 3. p. 443.
3. Mehring Franz: *Karl-Marx: The Story of His Life,* p. 152. George Allen and Unwin Ltd. London. (1948).
4. Sdobnikov Yuri: Karl Marx: A Biography, pp. 351-352. Progress Publishers, Moscow, (1973).
5. Sdobnikov Yuri: Karl-Marx: A Biography, p. 192.
6. For details see,Mehring Franz: Karl Marx: The Story of his life. p. 389.
7. *Ibid.,* p. 390.
8. *Ibid.,* p. 391
9. Sdobnikov Yuri: Krl-Marx: A Biography. p. 458.
10. Johson Gerald W. Communism: *A Study of Revolution*. p. 12. William Morrow and Co. Park Avenue, New York. (1966).
11. Sdobnikov Yuri: Karl-Marx: A Biography, p. 324.
12. *Ibid.,* p. 325.
13. *Ibid.,* p. 327.
14. For details see 'American Government and Politics' by Zink, Penniman and Hathorn. pp. 24-26. (1953).

14(a) Sdobnikov Yuri. *Karl Marx: A Biography*. p. 348.

14(b) *Ibid.,* p. 345.

15. Marx-Engels: *The Socialist Revolution*. p. 106. Progress Publishers, Moscow. (1978).

15(a) Hussain Iqbal (Ed.) Karl-Marx on India. pp. 266-267. Aligarh Historians Society Tulika Books Shahpur Jat, New Delhi. (2006).

16. Marx-Engles: Manifesto of The Communist Party, p. 22.
17. Lenin: The State and Revolution. p. 42.
18. *Ibid.,* p. 52.

18(a) Mathew Thomas: Ambedkar: *Reform or Revolution*, p. 160. Segment Books, Newn 1991.

19. Sdobnikov Yuri: Karl-Marx: pp.125-126.
20. *Ibid.,* p. 126.
21. *Ibid.,* p. 175.
22. Mehring Franz; *Karl-Marx: The Story of his Life,* p. 154.
23. For details see: *Karl Marx : A Biography*: by Yuri Sdobnikov, pp. 245 to 248.
24. Mehring Franz: *Karl Marx: The Story of his Life*. p. 321.
25. Sdobnikov Yuri: *Karl Marx: A Biography*: p. 416.
26. *Ibid.,* p. 512.

27. Volkov Genrikh: *Birth of a Genius*: p. 186.
28. Mehring Franz: *Karl Marx: The Story of his Life* pp. 334-335.
29. Based on the philosphy of Dr.Babasaheb Ambedkar and Lord Buddha.
30. Keer Dhananjay: *Dr. Ambedkar: Life and Mission* p. 42. Popular Prakashan, Bombay. (Edn.1971).
31. Khairmode C.B. Dr. Bhimrao Ramji Ambedkar: Charitra, Vol. II. p. 106.
    Boudhajan Panchayat Samiti, Parel, Mumbai (1958).
32. Keer Dhananjay: *Dr. Ambedkar: Life and Mision*. p. 60.
33. Bahishkrit Bharat, 20-5-1927:
34. For details see, '*What Path Salvation.*' Address delivered on 31st May 1936 at Mahar Conference at Bombay. pp.11-71. Thus Spoke Ambedkar Vol. IV. Edited by Bhagwan Das. (1980) also see Dhananjay Keers "Dr. Ambedkar: *Life and Mission*, pp. 273, 74, 75.
35. Ganjare M.F.Bhashane: Vol. III. p. 74.
36. *Ibid.*, p. 125.
37. *Ibid.*, p. 134.
38. *Ibid.*, pp. 132-135.
39. DBAWS. Vol. I, p. 80.
40. DBAWS. Vol. II, p. 131.
41. *Ibid.*, p. 134.
42. Keer Dhananjay: *Dr. Ambedkar: Life and Mission*, p. 112.
43. DBAWS. Vol. II, p. 84.
44. *Ibid.*, p. 101.
45. *Ibid.*, p. 100.
46. *Ibid.*, p. 101.
47. Narwade S.S. History of Independent Labour Party, p. 134. Vishwakarma Publication, A-396, Kansai Rtd., Subhas Tekadi, Ulhasnagar, Dist. Thane. (1997).
48. DBAWS: Vol. 2. p. 94.
49. Ganjare M.F.: Bhashane. pp. 149-152.
50. DBAWS: Vol. 2, p. 166.
51. Keer Dhanajay: *Dr. Ambedkar: Life and Mission*. pp. 303-305.
52. DBAWS: Vol. 2, p. 207.
53. Article by Dilip M. Dhiwal in Dr. B.R. Ambedkar. Edited by K.N. Kadam. (1993) p. 182.
54. *Ibid.*, p. 192.
55. DBAWS. Vol. 18 (3). p. 244. (2002).
    (Speech delivered on the occasion of foundation laying

ceremony of Milind College at Aurangabad on 01-09-1951.

56. Keer Dhananjay: *Dr. Ambedkar: Life and Mission*. p. 124.
57. DBAWS: Vol.2: p. 465.
58. DBAWS: Vol.1: pp. 429-430.
59. For details see 'Political Thought of Dr. Babasaheb Ambedkar' by Dr. R.K. Kshirsagar, Chapter 9, "Thoughts on Representation of the Scheduled Castes". pp. 72-88.
Intellectual Publishing House, "Darya Ganj, Ansari Road, New Delhi.(1992)
60. Johnson G.W. Communism: A Study of Revolution. p. 33. William Morrow and Co. 425 Park Avenue South, New York. (Edn.1966)
61. For details *see,* Dr. Bhimrao Ramji Ambedkar, Vol.7, by C.B. Khairmode. pp. 7-15.
Maharashtra Rajya Sahitye Sanscriti Mandal, Mumbai, (1985); and
"Political Thought of Dr. Babasaheb Ambedkar by Dr. R.K. Kshirsagar. pp. 91-98 (1992).
62. Keer Dhananjay: Dr. Ambedkar: Life and Mission. p. 325.
63. *Ibid.,* p. 303.
64. *Ibid.,* p. 343.
65. For details *see* Political thought of Dr. Babasaheb Ambedkar, by Dr. R.K. Kshirsagar. pp. 98-107.
66. *Ibid.,* p. 29
67. DBAWS: Vol.13: p. 327.

9

Observations

The study of Karl Marx and Babasaheb Ambedkar obviously reveals that both of them stand staunchly for the liberation of the suffering classes, but at the same time they stand naturally apart in respect of their individual life experiences, social atmosphere and perception, objectives and approaches to the concerned problem.

1. Karl Marx observed that, "the history of all litherto existing society is the history of class-struggle."[1] There has been constant conflict of interests between the Bourgeoisie and Proletariat Classes. So far as Indian situation is concerned the said statement seems to be irrelevant. Indian history is obviously the history of caste and communal struggle. The creation of *varna* and caste is the creation of the divisive mind of the Brahmanic forces. Therefore, contempt and hatred were deeply rooted in the very beginning of the Hindu society. This naturally gave rise to dissensions, rivalry and caste-war resulting in national cleavage.
2. Karl Marx gave materialistic interpretation of history. Accordingly the moving force in history was not 'spirit' or 'idea', but the relations in which men stood to each other in the process of production. Thus, the 'matter' is the prime mover in history. However, Babasaheb Ambedkar said that, history can not be made only by material forces. Historical changes are result of social, political, economic, religious and other forces. In his own words, "Man.... is a factor in the making of history and that environmental forces whether impersonal or social, if they are the first are not the last things."[2]

3. Karl Marx finds dialecticism and dynamism in history, but does not contemplate the possibility of the same after revolution. In the words of Watkins, "he also gave the Proletarians reason to believe that theirs was destined to be not just one revolution among many but a final and decisive achievement. In so doing he reached a degree of utopianism which outdates even the most optimistic hopes of his liberal predecessors."[3] Babasaheb Ambedkar being a true follower of Buddha never claims any thing to be infalliable and eternal. Society has to be dynamic in its attitude.

4. In the opinion of Karl Marx, the problem of the Proletariat was economic, whereas in the opinion of Babasaheb Ambedkar, the problem of the untouchables was obviously political rather than economic. The caste system generates the sense of superiority or inferiority in relation to others not because one caste is economically rich and other is poor, but because of one's birth in a particular caste which is either superior or inferior in the caste system as provided in the Dharma *Shastras*.

   While stating the specific nature of the problem of the untouchables, Babasaheb Ambedkar had very categorically said that, "we are often reminded that the problem of the depressed classes is a social problem and that its solution lies elsewhere than in politics. We take strong exception to this view."[4] Further, he said that, "self-respect is more important than the material gains. Our struggle is for honour, for self-respect, not only for the economic progress."[5]

   It seems that Marx was not fully aware of the Hindu Social Structure and the role of caste and 'untouchability' in the Indian history. To expect something arbitararily from Marx, which is not in his knowledge would be injustice on his part.

   While suggesting remedy on the economic ills of Proletariat, Karl Marx said that, "The proletariat must first of all acquire political supremacy."[6] Dr. Babasaheb Ambedkar also suggested the same remedy on the ills of the lower castes. He said that, "we can have one power and that is the political power. This power we must win, armed with this power we can protect the interests of our people."[7] Thus, so far as remedy on the problem of the proletariat as well as the 'Depressed Castes' is concerned the views of both the thinkers are identical.

5. So far as the way of attaining the power is concerned they differ in their opinion. Karl Marx states that 'ends' of the proletariat "can be attained only by the forcible overthrow of all existing social conditions. Let the ruling classes tremble at a communistic revolution."[8] However, Babasaheb Ambedkar believed in constitutional means. He thought that public opinion can be moulded by proper education and orientation.

6. Karl Marx thought that the state being the protector of vested interests of the Bourgioisie class, it has to be smashed by revolution. However, from the destruction of remnants of the Bourgioisie state to the formation of Communist state, there would be dictatorship of the Proletariat for a short duration of transition. However, he was not very much clear as to what happens subsequently. On the other hand, Babasaheb Ambedkar thinks to retain the state, Constitution and democratic government and through them he wants to bring about the welfare state by establishing state socialism.

   State is undoubtedly a natural entity, but being non-organic in nature. it has no its own 'will' or 'consciousness', other than the will or consciousness of the men who form the government. If the people want change, they can constitutionally change the government. Neither it is needed nor it is appropriate to smash the state.

7. Karl Marx was a great rationalist. He had no faith in religion which takes the credulous masses towards

fictitious God, soul, heaven, hell, idol worship and superstitions. Having seen the havoc played by christian religion in Europe he came to the conclusion that religion is the opium of the people.[9] He states Explicity that communism abolishes all religion and all morality. Dr. Babasaheb Ambedkar also was very much antagonistic to Traditional Hinduism which favours, among others, inequality among the human beings on the basis of caste system. Eventually, he discarded Hinduism and embraced Buddhism which is basically rational and which believes in liberty, equality and fraternity. Buddha's doctrine of 'Dependent Origination'[10] has really investigated the principle behind the phenomenal world and discarded the God.

Karl Marx firmly believed that as soon the material conditions change, the mind would accept a new value system. He, however visualised a contented man whose physical wants are satisfied. He assumes that such a man would be able to develop his moral standard. But is it certain that such a man would develop his moral standard ? It may be true in some individual cases, but this phenomenon can not be generalised. Hence, Babasaheb Ambedkar wanted to give Buddhism, being a code of right conduct, for training the human mind in morality; self-restraint and positive thinking. Thus, he contemplates material as well as moral development of the human beings.

8. Karl Marx, thought that mind is the product of material forces. Following Buddha Dr. Babasaheb Ambedkar stated that, "In every element the primal element is mind. Mind is pre-emient."[11] He thought that, mind should be kept far away from ignorance and impure thoughts. There was "matter" before the scientific investigations. However, due to want of inquisitive 'mind', there were not investigations and no scientific development. When the scientist or researchers applied their mind to the particular phenomenon they could find out the 'cause' behind the 'effect.'

9. Both, Karl Marx and Babasaheb Ambedkar are not determinists or conformists. Both of them think that for human suffering or *Dukkha* there is a cause; and that cause is 'human' and not 'divine'. Marx thought that private property was the cause of suffering of the proletariat whereas Babasaheb Ambedkar thought that private property and religion were the causes of suffering of the weaker sections of the society in India. They could rationally discover the real cause of human suffering. They did not believe in any divine curse or fortune. Both of them thought that there is proper remedy on the suffering.
10. However, there is distinction between them on the theory of 'base' and 'super-structure'. Karl Marx evidently contemplates that mode of production is the base and all the political and intellectual life is the super-structure. If the base is changed the whole superstructure would automatically change. On the other hand, Babasaheb Ambedkar, believing in Mahatma Phule, contemplates that 'Ignorance' (*Avidya*) is the base-cause, which could be removed by 'education' or knowledge and a new society could be formed.
11. Capitalism, contemplated by Marx, seems to be no more in existence at present. The capitalists now-a-days are operating with the help of many managers, technocrats, legal advisors and the whole paraphernalia. The 21st Century capitalism is a corporate capitalism different from the individualistic capitalism of 19th century. Several laws regarding work-time, wages, safety and security, compensation, etc., are being implemented and supervised. Even the theory of 'surplus value' seems to be redundant. The industrialists can not appropriate the profit for their own whims. Now, the profit is proportionately distributed amongst the proprietors, share-holders or partners of the enterprise. The provisions made under the law of income tax, wealth tax, provident fund, insurance etc., will take out some

portion from the gross profit, which otherwise would have gone to the capitalists. Thus the margin of profit came down to a certain extent.

Of course, it does not mean that there is no profit, no wealth accumulation, no exploitation at all. It only means that there is considerable change in the 19th century capitalism and 21st century capitalism. The capitalists easily get the advise from the accountants, auditors, legal advisors and others for extracting maximum benefit. Therefore, capitalism is growing and poverty is also growing. The nature of capitalism has changed, but still it is in its full bloom. Therefore, in the light of changing situation, the working class has to be organised with a new strategy and with new instruments.

12. During the days of Marx there were altogether 28 States in Germany. They formed the German Empire in 1871. It was a autocratic state. People were under the influence of feudals, capitalists and the priestly class. Hence, Marx had no faith in the state machinery. Therefore, he thought that there ought to be dictatorship of proletariat, at least during the period of transition from capitalism to communism. Further, he states that the state will wither way. Again he asks the Communists to take the control of the state or government for the protection of egalitarian society.

During those days the democratic process was very slow. There were decision-making bodies but the franchise was limited and qualified. People having property were qualified to vote. Women were disqualified to vote."[12] Consequently, there was lack of representative government in the true sense. Moverover, constitutionalism is a later development. Therefore what Marx professed in those days was true.

During the days of Babasaheb Ambedkar the situation has changed considerably. Democratic process was developed, constitutionalism was prevailing, labour laws were brought into implementation, and there was remarkable change in science and technology. Therefore, Babasaheb Ambedkar has rightly thought that there was sufficient scope for welfare of the people in democracy. He thought democracy is a best form of government. Dictatorship is dictatorship whether it is by proletariat or by capitalists. He had utmost faith in liberty, equality and fraternity and there was possibility of these principles only in democracy. Therefore, he is admirer and protagonist of democracy.

13. In the process of production several factors like land, capital, labour, water, energy, raw material, planners etc., are necessarily involved. However, Marx gives primordial importance to labour power. On the other hand, Babasaheb Ambedkar takes into account the vital role of almost all the factors which are involved in the process of production. He tries to bring about a necessary equilibrium, co-ordination and mutual co-operation among all the factors.

14. In addition to the Proletariat Classes in the world and the backward castes in India, there are some other oppressed communities in different countries, such as Native Americans or American Indians, Mexican Americans or Chicanos, Afro-Americans or Blacks and Japanese Americans in America, Jews and Gypsies in France, Roma in Austria and Burakumin in Japan.[13] They are also in quest for justice. It is necessasry to bring awareness to them and bring them to the level of developed communities, culturally, economically and politically. Therefore, a suitable strategy has to be adopted which could be able to give them justice.

15. It is very much pertinent to remember that the philosophy of Karl Marx and Babasaheb Ambedkar is not a dogma, but a dynamic thought. They have given scientific solutions on the problems existing in their time. However, those scientific solutions ought not to be used as ready made solutions on prospective problems without much going into deep dignosis of the problem.

While talking to the Russian revolutionaries "Engels insisted that they should not just quote Marx's works but try to think as Marx would have thought in their place. He believed that only in this case the word "Marxist" had the right to exist."[14] It is a very important key to interpret the thoughts of Karl Marx. Accordingly, every word should reflect the 'Marxist' thought in the real perspective.

Same is true of Dr. Babasaheb Ambedkar also. It is pertinent to think as to what Babasaheb Ambedkar would have thought in a given situation. It is necessary to test those thoughts on the envil of scientific inquiry as to its truth of being Ambedkarite.

While interpreting the thoughts of any thinker necessary care has to be taken to differentiate what is said by him in a specific context or as a matter of strategy or on a spur of moment from what he contemplated to say.

16. With the major setback to communism coinciding with disintegration of Soviet Union in 1991, communism has started fading. China has retained communism but accepted membership of the world trade organisation, tilting towards liberalisation. Even they have reportedly allowed the capitalists and industrialists to be members of the Communist Party. How far it would go on sinking?

So far as Indian situation is concerned where caste, class and tradition exist communism can not rise up unless there is radical change in leadership and ideology. Caste is a stumbling block in its way, which the Communists could not overcome till now in interpreting ideology, and in applying it in practice.

In the present society, democratic values are highly popular and held in esteem. However, capitalists-oriented democracy devoid of social justice also became redundant and irrelevant. The exploited masses are in need of social justice. Gandhism can not bring social justice to them with its traditional and decadent philosophy. Taking into account the present nature and needs of the society a suitable philosophy has to be adopted. There ought to be strong alliance between the industrial labour, agricultural labour, workingmen and weaker sections of the society.

The philosophy which is rational, safer and sure, democratic, egalitarian, judicious and promoting moral and material advancement of the people would be preferable. It seems that Ambedkarism fulfils these criteria of a suitable philosophy.

Notes and References

1. Marx-Engels: *Manifesto of the Communist Party*. p. 40 (2012).
2. DBAWS. Vol. 1. p. 213.
3. Watkins F.M. *The Age of Ideology*: p. 52.
4. DBAWS. Vol. 2. p. 506.
5. *Ibid,*. Vol. II, p. 145.
   Bhagwan Das (Ed.) *Thus, Spoke Ambedkar*. Vol. II, p. 145.
6. Marx-Engels: *Manifesto*. p. 71.
7. Bhagwan Das (Ed.) *Thus Spoke Ambedkar*, Vol. II. p. 35.
8. Marx-Engels: *Manifesto*. p. 96.
9. Marx-Engels: *Contribution to the Critique of Hegels' Philosophy of Law*, p. 175. Vol. 3.
   Progress Publishers, Moscow. (1975).
10. For details see DBAWS.Vol. II. p. 255.
11. *Ibid.*, p. 360.
12. New Zealand became the first country in the world to grant women the right to vote in 1893.
13. For details see 'Long-suffering Brothers and Sisters, Unite! p. 142-219. Published by Buruku Liberation Research Institute, Osaka, Japan (1981).
14. Volkov Genrikh: *Birth of a Genius*: p. 215.
    Progress Publishers, Moscow (1978).

Bibliography

Ahir D.C. Dr. Ambedkar on Buddhism, (1982), Siddharth Publication, PES, Anand Bhavan, Fort, Mumbai.

Atre Trimbak Narayan: Gaon Gada. (1915) Varada, Pune.

Banaji D.A. Slavery in British India (1933), Taraporwala Bombay

Barmenkov A. Freedom of Conscience in the USSR (1979), Progress Publishers, Moscow.

Bhatia H.L., History of Economic Thought (1977) Vikas Publishing Jangpura, New Delhi.

Buhler G. Laws of Manu (1886; 1964), Motilal Banarasidas, Delhi.

Burlatsky (Ed.) Fundamentals of Marxist-Leninist Philosophy. (1985). Progress Publishers, Moscow.

Das Bhagwan : Thus Spoke Ambedkar Vol. I-IV.
___ Main Bhangi Hun :
Gautam Book Centere, Shahadara, Delhi.

Desai A.R. : The Marxist Theory of State. (1979)., Shah Memorial Trust, Taikalwadi Rtd., Mumbai.

Doyle Phyllis : A History of Political Thought (1933)., Jonathan Cape, London.

Dongre M.K.: Economic Thoughts of Dr. Babasaheb Ambedkar (1974). Ambedkar Samaj Publication, Nagpur.

Dr. Babasaheb Ambedkar: Writings and Speeches : Education Department of Government of Maharashtra, Mumbai, Vol.I to 20.

Ghurye G.S.: Caste, Class and Occupations (1961)., Popular Book Depot, Bombay.

Ganjare M.F.: Dr. Babasaheb Ambedkar: Bhashane. Vol. (1-7).

George H. Sabine: A History of Political Theory (1937-1950). Oxford and IBH Pub. Co. Calcutta.

Goyanka Satyanarayan : Kya Buddha Nastik The? (2008) Vipassana Vishodkan Vinyas, Dhammagiri, Igatpuri.

Gokhale Pradeep (Ed) : The Philosophy of Dr. B.R. Ambedkar: (2008) Sugawa Prakashan, Pune.

Hadekar D.Y.: Buddhacha Bhoutikvad, (2008) Sugawa Prakashan, Pune.

Huberman Leo: Introduction to Socialism (1968) Progressive Book Depot, Paharganj, New Delhi.

Hunt Carew: The Theory and Practice of Communism.

Hussain Iqbal (Ed). Karl Marx on India (2006). Tulika Books Shapur, New Delhi.

Hutton J.H. : Caste in India (1969). Oxford University Press, London.

Johnson Gerald: Communism: A Study of Revolution (1964). Park Avenue South, New York.

Keer Dhananjay: Dr. Ambedkar: Life and Mission (1971). Popular Prakashan, Tardeo Rtd., Mumbai.

Keer-Malashe : Mahatma Phule : Samagra Vangmaya (1980). Government of Maharashtra, Mumbai.

Khairmode C.B.: Dr. Bhimrao Ramji Ambedkar: Charitra. Vol. 1 12 Dr. Ambedkar Education Society, Mumbai.

Kasabe Raosaheb: Ambedkar Ani Marx (2006). Sugava Prakashan, Pune.

Kadam K.N.: Dr. Babasaheb Ambedkar and Significance of his Movement (1991), Popular Prakashan, Mumbai.

Kosare H.L.: Vidarbhatil Dalit Chalvalicha Itihas (1984). Dnyandeep Prakashan, Nagpur.

Kausalyayan Anand: Boudh Dharma Ek Buddhivadi Adhyayan (1993).

Kshirsagar R.K.: Political Thought of Dr. Babasaheb Ambedkar (1992). Intellectual Publishing House, Darya Ganj, New Delhi.

Kosambi D.D. : Exhasperating Essays (1977), Indian Book Exchange, Calcutta.

Karkhanis Sarita : Marxvad Mhanaje Kay ? (1960), Lokvangmaya Griha, Prabhadevi, Mumbai.

Lenin: Collected Works.

Lynch Owen M.: The Politics of Untouchability (1974). National Publishing House, Darya Ganj, New Delhi.

Mehring Franz : Karl Marx: The Story of his Life (1948). George Allen and Unwin Ltd., London.

Mangudkar M.P.: Dr. Ambedkar: Parliament and Democracy (1976), Madiwale Colony, Poona.

Marx Karl: Manifesto of the Communist Party (2012), People Publishing House (P) Ltd. New Delhi.

Mill J.S.: On Liberty (1962), Colins Press, London.

Mahar Michael (Ed) : The Untouchables in Contemporary India. (1972), University of Arizona, U.S.

Mathew Thomas: Ambedkar: Reform or Revolution (1991), Segment Books, New Delhi.
__Re-reading Ambedkar (2007
Samyak Prakashan, Paschimpuri, New Delhi.

Miliband Ralph : Class Power and State Power (1983) 15, Greek Street, London.

Misra B.: Capitalism, Socialism and Planning (1982). Oxford & IBH Publishing Co. New Delhi.

Murthy K. Sachitanand : Nagarjuna (1983) National Book Trust of India, New Delhi.

Malkani N.R.: Clean People and Unclean Country (1965).
Narasu P. Lakshmi: The Essence of Buddhism (2002) Buddha Bhoomi Prakashan, Nagpur.

Narwade S.S.: History of Independent Labour Party (1977) Vishwakarma Pub. Subhash Tekadi, Ulhasnagar, Thane.

Nim Hotilal: Thought on Dr. Ambedkar (1969) Anand Sahitye, Sadan, Cantt. Aligarh.

O'Malley L.S.S.: Indian Caste Customs. (Edn.1974) S.Chand and Co. New Delhi.

Omvedt Gail: Cultural Revolt in Colonial Society (1976) Scientific Socialist Ed. Trust, Bombay.

Patil Vishwas: Karl Marx: Vyakti Ani Vichar (2010) Padma Gandha Prakashan, Pune.

Pradhan G.R.: Untouchable Workers of Bombay City (1938) Karnataka Publishing House, Bombay.

Prasad Bimla (Ed): Socialism, Sarvodaya and Democracy (1964) Asia Publishing House, Mumbai.

Padhye Prabhakar: Manav Ani-Marx (1980). Shri Vidya Prakashan, Pune.

Prasad A.K.: Devadasi System in Ancient India (1990). H.K. Publishers, Shakti Nagar Ext., Delhi.

Rajanish : Samajwadse Savadhan (1970). Star Publications, Asaf Ali Road, New Delhi.

Rajasekharia A.M.: B.R. Ambedkar: The Politics of Emancipation.

Ram Nandu: Beyond Ambedkar (1995).

Saradamoni K.: Divided Poor: A Study of a Keala Village (1981) Ajanta Pub. Delhi.

Sharma R.P.: Modern Western Political Thought (1976). Sterling Publishers (P) Ltd., New Dehi.

Singh Yogendra : Modernisation of Indian Tradition (1986). Rawat Publications, Jawahar Nagar, Jaipur.

Sanjana J.E. : Caste and Out-caste (1946). Thacker and Co. Ltd. Bombay.

Shyamlal: The Bhangi in Transition (1984). Inter-India Publications, New Delhi.

Sanskrityayan Rahul: (Ed.) Buddhism: The Marxit Approach, (1970), People's Pub. House, Delhi.

Shetty V.T. Rajshekhar: How Marx failed in Hindu India. (1978) Karnataka Rationalist Association, Bangalore.

Swami Dharma Theerth Maharaj: History of Hindu Imperialism (1941, 1946), Happy Home Pub. Gandhi Nagar, Delhi.

Sharma T.R.: Relevance of Marxism in The Contemporary World (1990), Patriot Pub. Laxmi Nagar, Delhi.

Stepanova E.: Short Biography of Karl Marx (Edn.1968) Progress Publishers, Moscow.

Tope T.K.: Constitutional Law of India (1982), Easteem Book Co. Lucknow.

Volkov Genrikh: Birth of a Genious (1978), Progress Pub. Moscow.

Walkins Fredrick: The Age of Ideology (1965), Prentice-Hall of India, New Delhi.

Yuri Sdobnikov: Karl Marx: A Biography (1973). Progress Pub. Moscow.

— Long-Suffering Brothers and Sisters Unite, (1981). Buraku Liberation Research Institute Kubyoshi, Naniwaku, Osaka City, Japan.

Veermani K.: The History of the Struggle for Social and Communal Justice in Tamil Nadu (1981)
Dravidar Kazhagam Publications, Chennai.

Index

A

C

D

J

K

L

S

W

Z